From *Naked Repub*

"Nobody likes beheadings."
—President George W. Bush,
March 20, 2006, referring to TV images of Iraq war

"It's amazing that so many kids turn out to be fairly
normal, considering the weird socialization
they get in public schools."
—Senator Rick Santorum, *It Takes a Family*

"Gay marriage should be between a man and a woman."
—Governor Arnold Schwarzenegger

"Nothing is more important in the face of a war
than cutting taxes."
—Representative Tom DeLay

"I don't think people understand quite what motivates
political giving anyway. Believe it or not, the main thing
that motivates it is friendships, I think."
—Representative John Doolittle,
on taking money from Jack Abramoff

"I've been to Europe once. I don't have to go again."
—Representative Dick Armey

"The internet is not something you just dump something on.
It's not a truck. It's a series of tubes."
—Senator Ted Stevens

"I did everything but drink the bong water."
—Representative Dana Rohrabacher

NAKED
REPUBLICANS

NAKED
REPUBLICANS

A Full-frontal Exposure
of Right-wing
Hypocrisy
and Greed

Shelley
Lewis

VILLARD
NEW YORK

Published in the United States by Villard Books, an imprint of The Random
House Publishing Group, a division of Random House, Inc., New York.

VILLARD and "V" CIRCLED Design are registered trademarks
of Random House, Inc.

ISBN 0-8129-7691-6

Printed in the United States of America

www.villard.com

246897531

First Edition

Book design by Susan Turner

Naked Republicans is dedicated to the loyal listeners of Air America Radio (especially *Morning Sedition* and *Unfiltered*); to the brilliant, funny, fierce liberal bloggers who form the Resistance; and finally, to the honest politicians of both parties still trying to serve with integrity. Maybe the four of us can have lunch one day real soon.

When they call the roll in the Senate,
the senators do not know whether to answer
"present" or "not guilty."

—THEODORE ROOSEVELT,
twenty-sixth president of the United States

CONTENTS

APOCALYPSE NOW, DAMN IT

So much has been accomplished in the six years since George W. Bush (the Decider) ran for president promising to restore honesty and integrity to the Oval Office. He phonied up a reason to attack Iraq and dragged us into a war he can't get us out of; his top adviser, Karl Rove, became the target of a grand jury investigation; the vice president's chief of staff, Scooter Libby, was indicted for lying, and *Bush* turned out to be the guy who authorized Libby to leak; his chief of procurement was arrested on corruption charges; and his former top domestic policy adviser was arrested and accused of ripping off Target and Hecht's department stores. Oh, and Cheney shot a guy in the face.

At the other end of Pennsylvania Avenue, things are no better. The Senate majority leader is under investigation for possible insider trading involving family stock; Tom DeLay got indicted, got demoted, and then got out; a powerful congressman was sent to jail for accepting (no, make that *demanding*) bribes; and a corruption scandal is spreading like toxic ooze through the Republican House membership. No wonder they pray so much.

Look, we've waited six long years for the Rapture to come and take all the Republicans up to heaven where they can't hurt us anymore. (Well, maybe not *all* the Republicans—we're pretty sure the Bush twins aren't going.) But every day we check the skies to see whether Tom DeLay, Rick Santorum, Sam Brownback, and the rest of them are floating away, leaving only their pajamas behind in a crumpled heap on the floor. And so far, bupkus. No Apocalypse. No Rapture. The closest we've come is kooky Pat Robertson warning that God is going to smite a town that voted out a creationist school board, and then make it rain on Gay Day at Disney World.

It's so frustrating: They want to go and we want to be left behind. It would be so perfect. We'll take our chances with the Beast as he walks among us, creating hell on earth for the nonbelievers. (We've survived Cheney, after all. Hey, wait a minute . . .) Anyway, the Rapture just isn't happening, and we can't wait any longer. Work with us, people. What Would Jesus Do?

We're confident in saying he would vote to throw out the whole pack of crooks, unless he had to vote on a Diebold machine, and then he'd end up voting for the Republicans. But at least he'd try.

How did it come to this? We hate to point fingers, but some of you voted for the guy you thought you'd rather have a beer with, not realizing his corporate frat brothers would drop a roofie in your glass. When you came to, the environment had been raped, your wallet was empty, and gas cost four dollars a gallon.

If you picked up *Naked Republicans* expecting to see hot man-on-dog Santorum sex, or young, muscular self-flagellating Opus Dei priests, we're afraid you're going to be disappointed. The best we can offer is Denny Hastert cavorting with beautiful sweatshop workers on a Mariana Islands beach. (*Kidding*! That *so* didn't happen—and if it did, we'd spare you the picture.) No hot sex here, unless you get turned on by corruption, in which case you're probably a lobbyist. And if so, why are you reading this when you could be bribing some Republican congressman?

We're going to give you the who, what, why, and where of weaseldom. And believe us, it's only a sample of what's out there. We think of this book as a public service, a voter's guide to the corrupt, the liars, the hypocrites, and the dim. Please, *this* time, make them go away. Without further DeLay.

NAKED REPUBLICANS SYMBOL KEY

Crusader shields. Whether you're fighting the "War on Christians" or launching your own Crusade, you better have a shield to protect yourself.

Butterfly nets. Time to get back to the cuckoo's nest!

Sledgehammers. The bully's favorite tool for "gentle persuasion."

Pants on fire. As in "liar, liar, pants on fire." Because sometimes when you're lying by the seat of your pants, they'll spontaneously combust.

1 2 **3** 4 **5** 6 **7** 8 **9** 10   **Hypocrisy scale.** You didn't actually expect them to practice what they preach, did you?

Weasels. We hope the PETA folks don't think it's cruel to compare these furry fellas to Republicans.

Empty suits. They go perfectly with the empty heads.

Golden fighter jets. War is hell, unless you can make a nice profit on it.

PART ONE
THE WACKOS

They're Under God, Under Suspicion,
or Under Medical Supervision

WITH GOD ON OUR SIDE

(and You Know Which God We're Talking About)

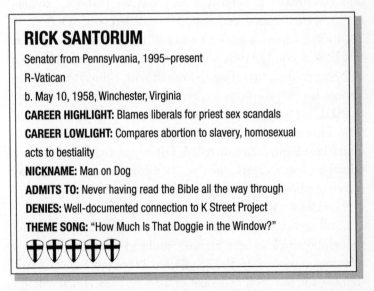

RICK SANTORUM

Senator from Pennsylvania, 1995–present

R-Vatican

b. May 10, 1958, Winchester, Virginia

CAREER HIGHLIGHT: Blames liberals for priest sex scandals

CAREER LOWLIGHT: Compares abortion to slavery, homosexual acts to bestiality

NICKNAME: Man on Dog

ADMITS TO: Never having read the Bible all the way through

DENIES: Well-documented connection to K Street Project

THEME SONG: "How Much Is That Doggie in the Window?"

It's amazing that so many kids turn out to be fairly normal, considering the weird socialization they get in public schools.

—RICK SANTORUM, *It Takes a Family*

It often seems that the junior senator from Pennsylvania should be on career-suicide watch. Nearly everything he's said or done in recent years, including writing a book, appears to be a desperate attempt to destroy himself.

When Rick Santorum began his national career in 1991 as a moralistic, way-holier-than-thou member of the House of Representatives, he probably had no idea that his name would become the punchline of a thousand kinky jokes. He was part of a group of conservative freshmen called the Gang of Seven who turned their righteous indignation on the Democratic House leadership. Like a pack of rabid accountants, they were fixated on the shoddy bookkeeping practices in the House. By today's standards, it seems petty—representatives were allowed to overdraw their accounts in the House bank, and some of them (*quelle surprise!*) took advantage of the system to bounce checks right and left. As far as we know, no civilian homes were bombed, and nobody was killed or maimed.

Riding that victory, Rick made it to the Senate, where at first he was simply a reliable tool of the lunatic fringe. But then he began to draw attention to himself with clumsy attempts to impose his moral worldview on the reality-based community. In 2001, he tried to force the teaching of "intelligent design" (also known as "magic") through an amendment to the No Child Left Behind Act. It failed, but he continued to support efforts to teach creationism while tub-thumping against gay marriage, abortion rights, SpongeBob SquarePants, and the rest of the evil liberal agenda.

Still, most casual observers of the theocracy-in-waiting thought of Rick as just another pinhead—until he gave his infamous interview to the Associated Press and achieved cult status as the cartoonlike mascot of the Christian Taliban. Here's the big moment:

SANTORUM: *In every society, the definition of marriage has not ever to my knowledge included homosexuality. That's not to pick on homosexuality. It's not, you know, man on child, man on dog, or whatever the case may be. It is one thing. And when you destroy that you have a dramatic impact on the quality—*

AP: *I'm sorry, I didn't think I was going to talk about "man on dog" with a United States senator, it's sort of freaking me out.*

And that's when the downward slide began. The butt (pun intended) of a thousand man-on-dog jokes, Rick saw nothing funny about it. Love the homosexual, hate the homosex, that was his motto. From there, it was an easy trip to authoring a book that blamed working mothers for most of the nation's problems. And who brainwashed them into abandoning their families?

The radical feminists succeeded in undermining the traditional family and convincing women that professional accomplishments are the key to happiness.

Another key to happiness would be having a job to earn enough money to provide food and shelter, but maybe that's just us. As for the earlier quote expressing his surprise that kids in public school can turn out to be normal, well, we're guessing he was speaking as a guy who'd been wedgied and stuffed into a lot of lockers in his public-school days.

And there was more. Rick blamed the Catholic pedophile priest scandal on liberals in Boston. Soon he made matters worse by flip-flopping on intelligent design.

When last we left Rick, he was urging voters to put Santorum bumper stickers on their cars to show their support for the troops. We know he's thinking about running for president, and we can only pray that he does. The nation needs to laugh more.

SAM BROWNBACK

Senator from Kansas, 1996–present

R–The Fellowship

b. September 12, 1956, Parker, Kansas

CAREER HIGHLIGHT: Elected to Senate with Pat Robertson's help

CAREER LOWLIGHT: Fined for campaign funding violation

NICKNAME: Saint Sam

ADMITS TO: Washing feet of a departing staffer as way of saying thanks

DENIES: Membership in spooky Opus Dei Catholic sect

THEME SONG: "Spirit in the Sky"

✝✝✝✝✝

Bless His Soles: Senator Washes Departing Aide's Feet

We're all in favor of senators being whipped—hell, we'd be happy to draw up a list of candidates. And if they want to do it to themselves, a little of the old self-flagellation, that's fine by us. We don't care if they sport barbed-wire thigh bracelets from time to time, or if they stick their tongues in a blender and set it on puree, for that matter. But when they recommend *we* do it, we have to draw the line.

We raise the matter of self-flagellation because Senator Brownback, Saint Sam, is believed to have been converted to Catholicism by a priest of the Opus Dei sect, a freaky quasi-cult whose practitioners sometimes enjoy a taste of the lash (see *The Da Vinci Code*). Saint Sam denies that he's a member, and we have no reason to doubt him—it's a sin to tell a lie, after all. But he does hang around with the kinds of religious wackos who identify with Opus Dei and other extremists. And make no mistake about it, he is coming to impose his religious beliefs on your government. (To say nothing of changing the vibe at a going-away party with that foot-washing thing.)

Saint Sam has already said he won't run for reelection to his Senate seat (although in Kansas, they won't have any trouble finding another wingnut to take his place). But he's making serious noises about running for the GOP presidential nomination in 2008, egged on by the unholy trinity of Pat Robertson, Randall Terry, and James Dobson. Can't you just see him at those candidate debates in New Hampshire, with eight or ten other Republican candidates scrambling to keep up with his God, gays, and abortion agenda? Before they're finished, the Republican Party platform will call for stoning stem-cell researchers.

But you don't have to wait until 2008—the *Make Room for Jesus* show is playing in Washington even as we speak. There's a bill that's been introduced twice, called the Constitution Restoration Act, which is designed to limit the power of the courts to prevent religion (and by that we mean Christianity) from being injected into official business. And it includes language that would prohibit a "renegade judge" from just ignoring the law. Yeah, yeah, we know, when you took civics class the three branches of government were equal, and there were checks and balances, blah blah blah. That is *so* twentieth-century thinking.

Saint Sam's first priority is controlling the reproductive organs of all women of childbearing age. He is the candidate of the "fetal citizens" (although we assume black fetal citizens would have their votes suppressed in Florida), and he talks of young people today who feel they are survivors of a holocaust because, unlike one-fourth of their age cohort, they were not aborted. They must be the same kids who survived the holocaust of Janet Jackson's Super Bowl boob flash only because of the efforts of Saint Sam. He has crusaded tirelessly to protect their tender morals when they watch television or listen to Howard Stern by demanding higher fines for "indecency."

No surprise, really—cleanliness is next to godliness. Still,

Saint Sam's holy pedicure raised a few eyebrows in D.C., not unlike the time John Ashcroft anointed himself with cooking oil for symbolic holiness and Wessonality. (Senator, next time try a simple gift card to Virgin Records.)

Ironically, Saint Sam says that if he runs for president he expects the public to respect his privacy about *his* religious beliefs. Given that he doesn't believe in a right to privacy for pregnant women or homosexuals, that seems a tad hypocritical. Let's just say potential voters might want to know more about the Fellowship of Christian extremists he meets with weekly in Washington, and the legislation that comes to him and his pals while they're praying.

The neocon dream of making the Middle East more like America seems to have backfired—the United States is looking more like Iran every year. What's next, a chain of Opus Dei's Inns?

TOM COBURN

Senator from Oklahoma, 2004–present

R–Nutjob

b. March 14, 1948, Casper, Wyoming

CAREER HIGHLIGHT: Claiming "gay agenda" is greatest threat to U.S.

CAREER LOWLIGHT: Protesting NBC's showing of *Schindler's List*

NICKNAMES: Dr. Don't; The Other Idiot from Oklahoma

ADMITS TO: Showing gross-out STD instructional films to staffers at lunchtime

DENIES: Sterilizing a female patient without her consent and defrauding Medicaid to pay for it

THEME SONG: "Girls Just Want to Have Fun"

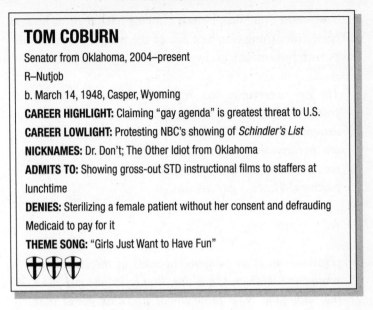

There are not many normal people up here.

—SENATOR TOM COBURN, speaking of his Washington colleagues

It's possible that that statement is the only thing Dr. Coburn has ever said that we'd agree with. Maybe you watched the Senate confirmation hearings of John Roberts in September 2005. (Then again, maybe you have a life.) If you weren't watching, you missed a very strange moment that occurred on the first day, when Oklahoma's own Doctor Senator Tom Coburn put down his crossword puzzle (really—there are pictures of him with it) and took his turn at the microphone. Apropos of nothing, he declared:

> *When I ponder our country and its greatness, its weaknesses, its potential, my heart aches for less divisiveness, less polarization, less finger-pointing, less bitterness, less mindless partisanship, which at times sounds almost hateful to the ear of Americans.*

The weird thing was, he was choking back tears as he said it. The weirder thing was, he's one of the people filling the airwaves with bitterness and divisiveness. Like when he said:

The gay community has infiltrated the very centers of power in every area across this country, and they wield extreme power. . . . That agenda is the greatest threat to our freedom that we face today. Why do you think we see the rationalization for abortion and multiple sexual partners? That's a gay agenda.

And:

[L]esbianism is so rampant in some of the schools in southeast Oklahoma that they'll only let one girl go to the bathroom. Now think about it. Think about that issue. How is it that that's happened to us? (Answer: It hasn't. The story was made up.)

Plus:

Global warming is just a lot of crap.

And of course:

I favor the death penalty for abortionists and other people who take life.

But how about:

Do you realize that if all those children had not been aborted, we wouldn't have any trouble with Medicare and Social Security today? That's another forty-one million people.

Wow, why didn't Paul Krugman think of that last one? No wonder Tom favors the death penalty for doctors who perform abortions.

Doctors who tie the tubes of minors without getting their consent . . . well, that's another story. A true story, but one that Tom would tell you was just an unfortunate mistake. He says the young lady in question gave him oral consent, but not written. She says she did nothing of the kind. Either way, he billed Medicaid for the procedure even though she wasn't eligible for it.

Maybe it was all just a simple misunderstanding.

Come to think of it, we wonder if there aren't a whole lot of things Dr. Don't misunderstands. Like when he told some women that not only are silicone breast implants safe, but women who have them are healthier than women who have real breasts (and are obliged to go on dates with the boobs they've got, not the ones they'd like to have, to paraphrase Rummy?).

And there was the crazy rant about showing *Schindler's List* on television. Dr. Coburn described it as "an all-time low, with full frontal nudity, violence, and profanity being shown in our homes."

Sort of conjures up a *Clockwork Orange* scenario, with poor Tom forced to sit in front of a TV set, eyes clamped wide open, while *Schindler's List* plays over and over, doesn't it?

Eventually, Coburn admitted he was wrong and apologized.

While he's no fan of *Schindler's List*, Coburn apparently takes great pleasure in showing congressional staffers a little drama called *Revenge of the STDs*. It's an exciting instructional slide show featuring *Star Wars* music and characters that very graphically depicts the havoc wreaked upon genitals by sexually transmitted diseases. The screening is an annual event, complete with pizza. At some viewings women have been reported to have run from the room gagging. Vote him out they should, as Yoda would say.

We don't know what Dr. Coburn's parents did to him when he was a lad growing up in Oklahoma, but it must have been awful. Maybe he caught them "dancing" late one night. Whatever . . . he's one of the wingnuts pulling the Republican Party even further to the right. We can only hope the people of Oklahoma will realize they are the only state in the nation with a worse senator than James Inhofe (their other senator). Please read on.

JAMES INHOFE

Senator from Oklahoma, 1994–present

R–The Holy Land

b. November 17, 1934, Des Moines, Iowa

CAREER HIGHLIGHT: Called the EPA "a Gestapo agency"

CAREER LOWLIGHT: Outraged over outrage at Abu Ghraib

NICKNAMES: Torquemada; The Other Nutjob from Oklahoma

ADMITS TO: Opposing federal holiday for Dr. Martin Luther King, Jr.

DENIES: Existence of global warming

THEME SONG: "King of Pain"

✝✝✝

One of the reasons I believe the spiritual door was opened for an attack against the United States of America is that the policy of our government has been to ask the Israelis, and demand it with pressure, not to retaliate in a significant way against the terrorist strikes that have been launched against them.

—JAMES INHOFE, March 2002

Next Will Senator Tell Abu Ghraib Victims "Walk It Off"?

It's kind of amazing when you think about it: Oklahoma has sent to the Senate not one, but two fanatical wackbags. One is afraid of gay people, the other is afraid of winding up on the business end of one of God's lightning bolts. And that gentleman is the senior senator, Jim Inhofe.

You see, America? We had it coming on 9/11. God was mighty pissed off at us for not letting Israel occupy all the land He gave them back in the day. Yes, that is the actual "thought" process of Senator James Inhofe. And while we are grateful that he didn't blame 9/11 on the feminists, lesbians, and abortionists, as Jerry Falwell did, we just aren't sure it was God's special wake-up call to those hoping for a deal between the Israelis and Palestinians. Maybe we're not sufficiently pious, but we blame 9/11 on Osama bin Laden.

The senator must have sensed we'd be all skeptical and snarky, because he went on to give seven reasons why Israel is supposed to have all of the Holy Land, climaxing with "Because God said so." No joke. You can look it up in the *Congressional Record* if you don't believe us. There you'll find lots of other tasty bits of wisdom from the Tulsa 'toon. Like the time he blocked a Clinton administration ambassadorship appointment for James Hormel because he's gay. When President Clinton made a recess appointment to get Hormel into his new job, Inhofe threw a tantrum, threatening to block all of Clinton's future nominations.

You might also enjoy Senator Inhofe's thoughts about the prisoner abuse scandal at Abu Ghraib. In May 2004, at an Armed Services Committee hearing investigating whose idea it was to pile naked Iraqi prisoners into human pyramids, he said:

> *I'm probably not the only one up at this table that is more outraged by the outrage than we are by the treatment.*

Surprisingly, not one senator jumped in to say, "Yeah, me too." He actually *was* the only one more outraged by the outrage than by the treatment.

Senator Torquemada's attitudes about torture seem to harken back to a simpler time—the Middle Ages—and that's where his information about global warming was probably developed, too. He dismisses research proving global warming as just a bunch of tricky junk science, and in a Senate speech in July 2003 he said:

> *With all of the hysteria, all of the fear, all of the phony science, could it be that man-made global warming is the*

greatest hoax ever perpetrated on the American people?
It sure sounds like it.

Those remarks made him something of a global laughing-stock, but we have to wonder if Senator Inhofe is listening to an even higher power: the energy industry.

People from oil, gas, and electricity companies are his biggest campaign contributors, to the tune of hundreds of thousands of dollars. He tried to tack language to allow oil drilling in the Arctic National Wildlife Refuge onto an emergency funding bill right after 9/11. Maybe it's just a coincidence that he described the EPA as "a Gestapo agency," or that he's voted against every environmental protection bill he's ever seen.

On the other hand, he's probably betting on Armageddon coming any day, so why clean the place up?

Won't somebody please send this Okie back to Muskogee?

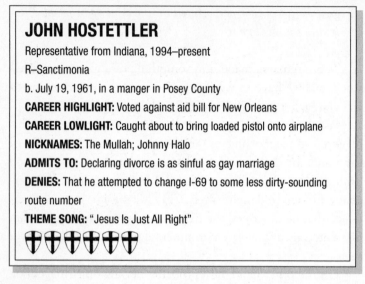

JOHN HOSTETTLER

Representative from Indiana, 1994–present

R–Sanctimonia

b. July 19, 1961, in a manger in Posey County

CAREER HIGHLIGHT: Voted against aid bill for New Orleans

CAREER LOWLIGHT: Caught about to bring loaded pistol onto airplane

NICKNAMES: The Mullah; Johnny Halo

ADMITS TO: Declaring divorce is as sinful as gay marriage

DENIES: That he attempted to change I-69 to some less dirty-sounding route number

THEME SONG: "Jesus Is Just All Right"

I hope to influence others to apply Christian principles to government.

—JOHN HOSTETTLER

Congressman Packs Gun;
Look Out, All You "Christ-Hating Democrats"

It's hard to decide just which leader of the impending Theocratic States of America is the most Jesus-loving—but whatever you do, don't forget to consider Congressman John Hostettler. After all, he was awarded the 2004 Distinguished Christian Statesman award, promising to infuse the government with Christian principles. Unless, of course, the Christian principles apply to governing poor black people in New Orleans. In that case, you'd better have a lot of faith, and plenty of hope, 'cause there won't be much charity, at least not from John Hostettler. He was one of eleven Republicans who voted against emergency aid to New Orleans after Katrina. He feared there'd be fraud and rip-offs, which would be a sin.

Not only did he feel okay screwing poor people who live in

the South, he somehow managed to ignore his own constituents in their time of need. When a devastating tornado hit
his home district a few months after Katrina (and we're not
going to go all Pat Robertson on you and say it was God getting
even), Johnny Halo opted not to go help out. He hunkered
down in his D.C. office for more than a week before showing
up to pick up some debris. He didn't want to get in the way, he
said. Of course, he did ask for federal funds for his district. He
may be a fanatic and a hypocrite, but he's not stupid.

Frankly it's a wonder Hostettler gets anything done, what
with having to fight off those Christian-hating Democrats all
the time. In June 2005, during a debate about a bill aimed at
preventing abusive religious proselytizing at the Air Force
Academy, he took to the floor to warn all the God-fearing
Christians:

> Like a moth to a flame the Democrats can't help them-
> selves when it comes to denigrating and demonizing
> Christians.

Hey, dude, you're the one dragging demons into the House
of Representatives. After half an hour of strong protests from
Democrats, Hostettler had to withdraw the remark and have it
stricken from the *Congressional Record.*

Honey, Have You Seen My Gun?

With "the long war on Christianity in America continuing,"
who could blame Congressman Hostettler for being armed at
all times? It was completely understandable when he attempted to board a plane at Louisville International Airport
with a loaded Glock 9mm pistol in his bag. He said he just forgot it was there. Who hasn't misplaced a loaded gun while they
were packing? A few months later, after he agreed to plead
guilty in return for a suspended sentence, he forgot something

else—to pay the court costs. A judge issued a bench warrant for his arrest. It was set aside a few hours later after he finally paid.

We can't help but think our congressman from Kandahar would just as soon establish religious courts to replace the ones we have. And the Taliban have nothing on him. Take divorce, for example. He and Jesus are opposed to it. Here's what Hostettler says about marriage:

> *The picture of marriage is the picture of Christian salvation. Any diminishing of that notion—whether homosexual marriage or any other degradation of marriage—is something we must fight in public policy.*

Marriage = Christian salvation, huh? Is it any wonder he had to deny publicly an Internet rumor that claimed he was planning to change the designation of Interstate 69 to something less sexually suggestive? It seems right up his alley.

Finally, we extend our sympathies to a group of breast cancer survivors who paid a visit to Johnny Halo. They thought they'd be discussing funding for breast cancer research, but he wanted to talk about the neolunatic myth that there's a link between abortion and breast cancer. The women were insulted, and when they later complained, he accused them of conducting a smear campaign against him. As for their feelings, Hostettler told a reporter, "I can't control what people feel. I can only control what I say."

If only.

2

LOON LAKE

Giving New Meaning to the Term "Political Asylum"

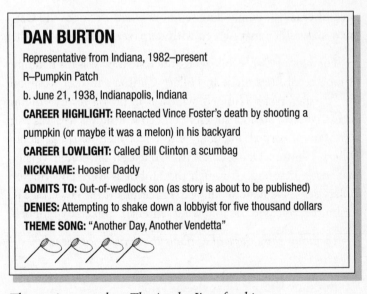

DAN BURTON

Representative from Indiana, 1982–present

R–Pumpkin Patch

b. June 21, 1938, Indianapolis, Indiana

CAREER HIGHLIGHT: Reenacted Vince Foster's death by shooting a pumpkin (or maybe it was a melon) in his backyard

CAREER LOWLIGHT: Called Bill Clinton a scumbag

NICKNAME: Hoosier Daddy

ADMITS TO: Out-of-wedlock son (as story is about to be published)

DENIES: Attempting to shake down a lobbyist for five thousand dollars

THEME SONG: "Another Day, Another Vendetta"

This guy's a scumbag. That's why I'm after him.

—DAN BURTON to *The Indianapolis Star* about Bill Clinton,

April 1998

Indiana has sent some true geniuses to Washington—Dan Quayle comes first to mind, of course, but for more than two decades of laugh-a-minute good times, we have to go with Congressman Dan Burton. From ethics charges to an embarrassing sex scandal, pretty much whatever Dan accused Mr. Clinton of doing, he's also been accused of. First elected to the House in 1982, he didn't achieve his full potential until 1996, when somehow he was given the chairmanship of the House Government Reform and Oversight Committee. From there he could zero in on the Clintons with Travis Bickle–like obsession, and he wasted no time.

His craziest move: Convinced that Clinton White House legal counsel Vince Foster was murdered, he placed a "head-like" object, believed to be a pumpkin, in his backyard and shot it. Something about gunshot noise—don't ask.

Second craziest: demanding to know whether Socks the Cat's fan mail was being answered with taxpayer dollars. (It wasn't.)

For a lot of Dan's colleagues, the last straw was his handling of tape recordings made of Hillary Clinton's former Rose law firm partner Webb Hubbell, who was in prison for overbilling clients. About 150 hours of Hubbell's conversations with his wife were tape recorded, including a few in which he spoke about Hillary Clinton. Dan's committee released an edited version that made it sound as though the Hubbells were covering up Hillary's involvement in billing irregularities at the law firm. The committee released the following sentence, spoken by Hubbell:

> *I will not raise these allegations that might open it up to Hillary.*

But they left out what else he said:

> *Okay, Hillary's not [vulnerable]. Hillary isn't. The only thing is, people say, "Why didn't she know what was*

going on?" And I wish she didn't pay any attention to what was going on in the firm. That's the gospel truth. She just had no idea what was going on. She didn't participate in any of this.

When his ham-handed (or in Dan's case maybe we should say pumpkin-headed) handling of the tape excerpts was revealed, he was forced to release all the tapes and do the manly thing, which was to fire an aide. (The aide was the notorious David Bossie, who was and still is a professional anti-Clinton, anti-Democrat agitator and alleged dirty trickster, so we didn't exactly feel bad for him.)

And what was the result of all of his investigations? Say it with us now: "Nothing." No evidence of crimes, misdemeanors, or improprieties.

Hoosier Daddy?

Too bad Dan's own record wasn't so clean. In 1998, in the midst of his moralistic crusade against virtually anyone who had anything to do with the Clinton administration, he was forced to admit that despite his 100 percent favorable rating from the Christian Coalition, he was no choirboy himself. He confirmed that he had an out-of-wedlock son. He says he's paid child support for the teenage boy, who does not use Burton's name (who could blame him?)

Dan says there's no truth to the story that he leaned a little too hard on a lobbyist for a campaign contribution. The lobbyist said Dan wanted five thousand dollars (at least!), and when he told him he couldn't get it, Dan warned him he'd better come up with it "if he knew what was good for him." We never did learn whether Hoosier Daddy carved the guy's face into a pumpkin and pretended he was Vince Foster.

DANA ROHRABACHER

Representative from California, 1988–present

R–Taliban

b. June 21, 1947, Coronado, California

CAREER HIGHLIGHT: Sponsored bill that would allow Arnold Schwarzenegger to run for President

CAREER LOWLIGHT: Conducted unauthorized and probably illegal negotiations with the Taliban before 9/11

NICKNAME: Surfer Dude

ADMITS TO: Being a huge pothead when he was young

DENIES: Lukewarm feelings (at best) for Israeli government

THEME SONG: "One Toke over the Line"

They're portraying Jack as a monster. I see him more as a good person who's done bad things.

    —DANA ROHRABACHER on Jack Abramoff, January 9, 2006

Congressman Rohrabacher is not about to abandon his friend just because Jack may be taking half the Republican Congress with him to jail. The two buddies go all the way back to the Reagan administration. Jack even hosted a baby shower for Dana and his wife Rhonda when they had their triplets. (Three little copies of Dana out there in the world? Do you think that's funny, God?)

But then, Congressman Surfer Dude has always been an excellent judge of character. He traveled to Afghanistan and met with the Taliban leadership in 1996, and darn it, he got a good feeling from those guys. Here's what *Washington Report on Middle East Affairs* (November/December 1996) reported:

Rohrabacher calls the sensational media reporting of the "harsh" imposition of strict Islamic behavior, with the underlying implication that this somehow threatens the West, "nonsense." He says the Taliban are devout tradi- tionalists, not terrorists or revolutionaries, and, in con- trast to the Iranians, they do not seem intent on exporting their beliefs.

Do you think maybe his judgment was impaired by all the pot he smoked as a kid? "I did everything but drink the bong water," he once said on *Politically Incorrect*.

In any case, he went back to Afghanistan and tried to nego- tiate with the Taliban a few years later (no, not to score some potent buds from the locals—apparently he was trying to set up an oil pipeline). It was all probably completely illegal, and it failed anyway.

The No Business in Show Business Award Goes to . . .

Luckily, Dana's used to rejection. He's been peddling screen- plays around Hollywood for thirty years, including one called "The French Doctoresse" that reportedly portrays Adolf Hitler rather sympathetically. (Hey, if he liked the Taliban, he's gotta *love* Hitler.) For some reason, no one wanted to produce that one, or his screenplay called "Baja" about a Vietnam veteran and a liberal graduate student who team up on an archaeologi- cal expedition in Mexico.

But then Rohrabacher met independent producer and ac- cused swindler Joseph Medawar, who paid him twenty-three thousand dollars for the option on "Baja." And then, no doubt by pure coincidence, he introduced Medawar to five Republi- can congressmen and staffers on the House Homeland Security Committee, which was super-helpful since Medawar was try- ing to produce a TV series about the Department of Homeland

Security. Medawar also got briefings from law enforcement officials who shared with him some of the inner workings of their agencies.

Rohrabacher denies doing anything wrong, but he returned the money just before Medawar pleaded guilty to scheming to swindle more than five million dollars from investors in his production company. Cowabunga, Surfer Dude. Gnarly luck.

TOM TANCREDO

Representative from Colorado, 1998–present

R–Borderline Personalities

b. December 20, 1945, Denver, Colorado

CAREER HIGHLIGHT: Getting screamed at by Karl Rove

CAREER LOWLIGHT: Trying to get an honor student deported because he was an illegal immigrant

NICKNAMES: The Vigilante; Tancretin

ADMITS TO: Having "limited skills"

DENIES: Bigotry, xenophobia

THEME SONG: "America, Fuck Yeah!"

Give me your tired, your poor, your huddled masses yearning to breathe free, / The wretched refuse of your teeming shore . . .
—EMMA LAZARUS, "The New Colossus"
(poem on the Statue of Liberty)

Massive immigration through porous borders combined with the corrosive effect of radical multiculturalism will not only determine what kind of nation we will be . . . it will determine if, indeed, we will be a nation at all.
—CONGRESSMAN TOM TANCREDO (whose grandfather sailed past the Statue of Liberty as he first entered the United States)

Yes, Tom Tancredo, right-wing immigration extremist, is the grandson of immigrants. To hear him speak of the corrosive effect of multiculturalism, you'd think his relatives were part of the welcoming party when the *Mayflower* landed. His Political Action Committee is called Team America, which he probably thinks sounds very patriotic but reminds us of Trey Parker and Matt Stone's puppet action movie, *Team America: World Police.* The theme song seems so right for Tancredo's team; it's called "America, Fuck Yeah!"

Somehow we doubt Tancredo and the Team America PAC president, Bay Buchanan, sing that song when they gather to plot ways to close America's borders. That image would be kind of funny if Tom Tancredo didn't proudly represent the growing movement to round up every illegal immigrant in the country and throw them all over a gigantic border fence.

Is It Too Late to Build a Moat on the Mexican Border?

Tom's biggest concern is that illegal Mexicans and others will overrun the country and "balkanize it," turning it into the United States of Serbo-Croatia. Thank God his border posse is riding hard to stop them. But don't think it's just those pesky Latino illegals who fry his frijoles. The Chinese are no better! They're trying to "extend their hegemony" by shipping off their people to our shores.

Hasta la Vista, Mecca

As for the Muslims, Tom Tancretin has a novel solution. He believes that the best response to another terrorist attack on the United States would be to "take out" Mecca, because it "might encourage moderate Muslims to start policing their own communities for extremists and jihadists." Maybe all this resentment stems from the days when Tom was a junior high school teacher dealing with the burden of forced bilingual education. It drove him *muy loco.* As a state legislator, he tried repeatedly to eliminate funding for bilingual education. When he first got to Congress, pretty much everybody ignored him. But like so many other Republicans who used 9/11 to advance their own agendas, Tom used the tragedy to crank up paranoia about America's borders. His Immigration Reform Caucus grew, and with it his power. Before long he was lecturing Karl Rove on the dangers of the president's immigration policies, and Team America was supporting two independent candidates who challenged Republicans he considered to be border pussies.

For his efforts, Karl Rove told him to stay the hell away from the White House, and Tom DeLay told him basically that he'd never eat lobbyist-funded lunch in this town again. Normally, anybody who gets reamed by both Karl Rove and Tom DeLay in the same decade is going to be a hero to us, but there's really nothing normal about Tom Tancredo. When he broke his promise to serve only three terms in Congress, he justified it with that drivel about radical multiculturalism. He went on to say:

> I find myself in a position of leadership with regard to this issue. . . . I represent [the] best hope for change. I dare not abandon this cause. The U.S. House of Representatives is the forum I have been given in which to use my limited skills for this purpose.

"Limited skills"? Finally—something we can agree on!

JOHN DOOLITTLE

Representative from California, 1991–present

R–Kookville

b. October 30, 1950, Glendale, California

CAREER HIGHLIGHT: Tried to replace FDR's profile with Reagan's head on the dime

CAREER LOWLIGHT: Accused liberals of being "anti-God bullies"

NICKNAME: Doo-De

ADMITS TO: Being one of the top recipients of Abramoff money

DENIES: Abramoff wanted anything in return for more than $100K

THEME SONG: "Paranoia"

He never asked me anything in return for that. I don't think people understand quite what motivates political giving anyway. Believe it or not, the main thing that motivates it is friendships, I think.

—JOHN DOOLITTLE, on taking money from Jack Abramoff

Up until recently, John Doolittle says, he always thought he was a pretty good judge of character. Take his friend Jack Abramoff, whom he saw as a fine, upstanding guy. Great sense of humor. Loved the whole orthodox Jewish thing. And it was just his good luck that Jack wanted to help him, without ever asking for anything in return. Of course the liberal media made something nasty out of a beautiful friendship. But don't worry, Doolittle's got their number:

> *[T]he same Beltway powerbrokers who have targeted me in the past—the labor union bosses, radical feminists and extreme environmentalists—are back again.*

Now that's a fundraising plea a Republican can get behind, right? Almost as good as scaring the bejeezus out of them:

A liberal front is under way to find God and all things pertaining to Him unconstitutional.

Wow. It must be scary to be John Doolittle. If it's not the "anti-God bullies," it's the radical feminists or the "eco-Marxists" who are out to get you.

John Doolittle, who was so closely affixed to Tom DeLay's bum that we call him Doo-De (the Lay is silent), is a complicated guy. He's a teetotaling, antigambling Mormon who takes money from liquor lobbies and Indian casinos. He came to Congress in 1991 and became one of the so-called Gang of Seven freshmen Republicans who accused the House Democratic leadership of corruption. And yet, so many of the seven gangstas are now facing ethics questions that we almost expect gang warfare to break out at any moment, complete with drive-bys and recording-studio shootouts.

After improving his street cred by taking down Congresswoman Mary Rose Oakar and others in the banking scandal, John decided he deserved to live a little larger. He began nagging the House leadership for perks that would make those violations look like penny-ante stuff. (Oh, wait, it *was* penny-ante stuff. But you get the point.) Doolittle petitioned for chauffeurs, errand boys (and girls) to do personal chores, and a hefty per diem for each member of Congress. The House leadership, after they stopped rolling their eyes, told him it wasn't going to happen. (He asked for the same stuff ten years later, by the way, and still got nowhere.)

Is it any surprise he joined dream date Tom DeLay in sponsoring legislation that would weaken campaign finance reform? The bill was called DeLay-Doolittle (say it out loud—it's delicious), words for Republicans to live by to this day. He's given

DeLay fifteen thousand dollars for his defense fund. As for his friend Jack Abramoff, who gave and gave and never wanted anything in return, well, here are some of the things Mr. Doolittle got:

- In 1999 he used Abramoff's skybox to entertain campaign donors, but he neglected to declare it. (Oops—awkward oversight!) When the whole Abramoff web began to unravel, Doo's name showed up on the skybox guest list.

- We also know that Doo-De got many thousands of dollars from Abramoff's tribal clients, and thousands more directly from Jack, and that he wrote letters in support of their causes.

- Mrs. Julie Doolittle was hired by Abramoff to do some event planning.

- The stickiest thing is that Doo steered millions of dollars in government contracts to a guy named Brent Wilkes, whose associates have contributed forty-six thousand dollars to Doo's campaign funds. Wilkes is called "co-conspirator #1" in the Duke Cunningham bribe case, and he has close ties to Tom DeLay. Oh, and did we mention the government contract was for a system the Pentagon said they didn't particularly want?

After blaming the liberal media for trying to get him, he said, "Hey, if you're concerned about me, investigate me." Brave words, Mr. Doolittle. Daring the feds. Truly gangsta.

3

THE BULLIES' PULPIT

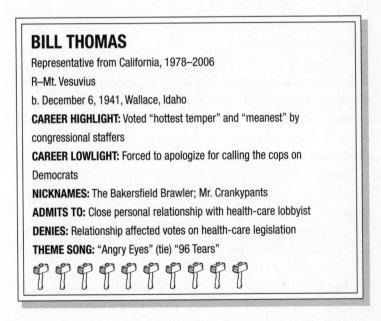

BILL THOMAS

Representative from California, 1978–2006

R–Mt. Vesuvius

b. December 6, 1941, Wallace, Idaho

CAREER HIGHLIGHT: Voted "hottest temper" and "meanest" by congressional staffers

CAREER LOWLIGHT: Forced to apologize for calling the cops on Democrats

NICKNAMES: The Bakersfield Brawler; Mr. Crankypants

ADMITS TO: Close personal relationship with health-care lobbyist

DENIES: Relationship affected votes on health-care legislation

THEME SONG: "Angry Eyes" (tie) "96 Tears"

Representative Bill Thomas is the Courtney Love of the United States Congress. One minute he's erupting in rage; the next, delivering a lip-quivering apology full of vows to clean up his act. Like Courtney, he embarrasses fans and foes alike with his crazy behavior. And while Courtney is given to assaulting fans with a microphone stand or an empty bottle, Big Bill is only slightly less physical in his angry eruptions.

In 1995 he went chest to chest with a seventy-five-year-old Democratic congressman, Sam Gibbons. Reporters looked on with bemusement as the confrontation escalated, finally ending with Bill screaming at Gibbons to let go of his tie. (Gibbons now jokes that he was going for Thomas's throat, not his tie.)

And that was before he became chairman of the powerful Ways and Means Committee (promising the GOP leadership that, yes, he would exercise a little more self-control). Sadly, despite the apologies and the promises, he just couldn't shake the rageaholic behavior.

In July 2003, he called the cops on Democrats who'd walked out of a hearing in disgust. The Capitol police declined his order to retrieve them. After days of resisting demands by his own party that he apologize, a shaken Bill Thomas publicly atoned for trying to turn the House into a police state. (That's the Justice Department's job, after all.)

Imagine Speaker Denny Hastert's surprise, then, when in October, just a few months later, he got a call from an angry President Bush, who complained that Thomas had gone medieval all over HHS Secretary Tommy Thompson's ass in some kind of closed-door meeting. Seems he was rude and shouted at him in front of other people.

But more disturbing than the rage was the awkward sight of Bill Thomas in tears. He could go all weepy when apologizing for making an ass of himself, but also at inexplicable moments, like during a Medicare vote, and during a news conference about a trade bill.

The Bakersfield Brawler has provided hours of entertainment, and now that he's announced his retirement, we're going to miss him. Bring some extra hankies for his going-away party. We have a feeling he's going to need them.

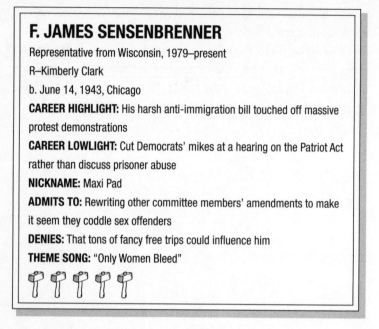

F. JAMES SENSENBRENNER

Representative from Wisconsin, 1979–present

R–Kimberly Clark

b. June 14, 1943, Chicago

CAREER HIGHLIGHT: His harsh anti-immigration bill touched off massive protest demonstrations

CAREER LOWLIGHT: Cut Democrats' mikes at a hearing on the Patriot Act rather than discuss prisoner abuse

NICKNAME: Maxi Pad

ADMITS TO: Rewriting other committee members' amendments to make it seem they coddle sex offenders

DENIES: That tons of fancy free trips could influence him

THEME SONG: "Only Women Bleed"

They'll flood our schools. Our health care system will collapse. And our social services system will end up being overtaxed. And we've got to get control of our borders because if we don't, we're going to see our economy collapse.

—JAMES SENSENBRENNER, on undocumented immigrants,
to Lou Dobbs

Heir to the Kotex Fortune Perpetually on the Rag

Meet Jim Sensenbrenner, the crankiest guy in Congress. But isn't it appropriate that a man whose great-grandfather invented Kotex would have male PMS his entire adult life? As the grouchy bully whose term as chairman of the Judiciary Committee has been a reign of terror, he must be especially proud of his harsh 2005 immigration bill that would make criminals out of millions of undocumented workers. When he's not making scary pronouncements about America's certain doom unless we round up and deport twelve million workers, he's basking in the warmth of some of his other accomplishments:

- He was one of eleven Republicans to vote against emergency aid to Katrina victims.

- He rejected Katrina victims' plea to be excluded from the draconian new bankruptcy laws.

- He turned a House hearing into Tiananmen Square, cutting off Democrats' microphones when they wanted to question a witness about prisoner abuse, and ordering C-SPAN to get out.

- He demanded that a federal judge overrule a three-judge panel's decision on a drug sentence. (The judge ignored him.)

- He attempted to criminalize broadcasters who allow indecency on the airwaves.

"Maxi Pad" Sensenbrenner is worth millions, and yet in December 1997 he bought a Quick Cash lottery ticket in Washington and won two hundred fifty thousand dollars, proving once again that God just isn't paying enough attention.

Besides tacking anti-immigration amendments onto everything that's crossed his desk except the office birthday card for his secretary, he's breaking new ground in the area of meddling in the judicial branch.

Sensenbrenner put the federal courts on notice that a little technicality like separation of powers won't stop him from trying to bully judges when the mood strikes. Legal observers say his meddling is inappropriate and may be an ethics violation (assuming the House has a conscious ethics panel). Big Jim also floated the idea of setting up an inspector general to keep an eye on activist judges.

Of all his acts of bullying and disrespecting his colleagues, his personal best was probably when he rewrote the summaries of Democratic amendments to the Child Interstate Abortion Notification Act. Unbeknownst to the committee members, his staff changed the descriptions to make them say that the Democrats' versions would protect child molesters and sexual predators. That was too crazy even for his fellow Republicans, and he had to change the language back.

Ich Bin ein Freeloader

Since he's always pissing somebody off in Washington, it's no surprise that Sensenbrenner gets out of Dodge a lot. Did we say "a lot"? We meant "the most." According to the watchdog group Political Moneyline, Air Maxi racked up the highest travel tab on private nickels—to the tune of two hundred thousand dollars over the past five years. And if you sneak a peek at his passport, you'll find it's got stamps from all kinds of exotic spots—Asia, Europe, the Middle East, and Vegas, to name just a few. For the past three years, he's gone to Berlin and Liechtenstein to discuss terrorism, which of course is a huge problem in Liechtenstein. Say, doesn't Kotex make those pads with "wings" for better security? Maybe he got his inspiration from the family business.

People in Wisconsin are sometimes called cheeseheads, but Big Jim's head makes us think of a different cow product—and it ain't dairy.

TED STEVENS

Senator from Alaska, 1968–Present

R–Oscar Mayer

b. November 18, 1923, Indianapolis, Indiana

CAREER HIGHLIGHT: Ted Stevens Anchorage International Airport

CAREER LOWLIGHT: Last-minute defeat of ANWR drilling

NICKNAMES: Ted Tantrum; Temper Ted

ADMITS TO: Being the King of Pork

DENIES: Sweetheart government contracts to favored lobbyists

THEME SONG: "We're on the Road to Nowhere"

I'm going to go to every one of your states, and I'm going to tell them what you've done. You've taken away from homeland security the one source of revenue that was new. . . . I'm sure that the senator from Washington [Cantwell] will enjoy my visits to Washington.

—TED STEVENS, on losing ANWR vote

When a man who is older than the moon has a tantrum, it isn't a pretty sight. On the other hand, when he's wearing an Incredible Hulk tie and threatening to destroy all the young whippersnappers around him, it's downright hysterical. The only way it might have been funnier is if he had been standing on his porch in his pajamas, brandishing a BB gun at the neighborhood kids cutting across his lawn.

Ted "Tantrum" Stevens clearly does not take defeat well. In this case, he watched as his decades-long dream of drilling for oil in the Arctic National Wildlife Refuge was blocked once again, despite his best efforts. Maybe it was payback for his snarling refusal to give up hundreds of millions in pork for his "bridge to nowhere" so that the money could be sent instead to Louisiana for post-Katrina repair work. He threatened to quit the Senate if that happened, and although it seemed to us to be a wonderful opportunity, his fellow senators backed down and let him keep the money for Alaska.

Senator Stevens wears the Pork King crown with pride; he makes no apology for making certain that Alaska rakes in more federal dollars per person than any other state. You might think that Ted Tantrum would have slowed down a little in 2005, given the nation's outrageous budget deficits, an endless war in Iraq, and the billions required to rebuild in the Gulf Coast after Katrina. You'd think he'd feel it was the patriotic thing to do. You would be *so* wrong.

Ted Tells Oil Execs: No Oath? No Problem!

Ted Tantrum is nothing if not consistent, and he is consistently a friend to the oil industry. That was evident when he refused to swear in five oil industry executives who'd come to testify before his committee. They had been called to talk about the suspicious spike in prices after Katrina, but Democrats wanted to know whether any of the execs were part of the secret Cheney energy task force meetings in 2001. When senators persisted in trying to require the execs to testify under oath, Ted Stevens blew another gasket, and snapped:

> That's the last we're going to hear about that, because it's out of order. I intend to be respectful of the position that these gentlemen hold.

And he was. With no worries about perjury, they all denied participating in the Cheney meetings, although evidence now shows that some of their companies did indeed meet with the task force.

It's hard to know which slab of bacon Stevens considers his

favorite. Maybe it's the Ted Stevens Anchorage International Airport. That has a nice ring to it. Or maybe it's the Alaska Airlines jet with a salmon painted on the side, to the tune of half a million dollars. Technically the money came from the Alaska Fisheries Marketing Board, but they got their money from the federal government. In fact, in the three years the Board has existed, they've gotten almost thirty million dollars from the federal government, courtesy of Ted Stevens. Oh, and guess who is the chairman of the Alaska Fisheries Marketing Board? Why, it's Ted's son, Ben. Funny, isn't it?

Be Afraid. Be Very Afraid

One last thought to help you sleep at night: Temper Ted is president pro tempore of the Senate. That means he's fourth in line for the presidency, and when you consider Boy George's propensity for pitching off his bike (or choking on pretzels) and Cheney's mechanical heart, we'd better all pray that Denny Hastert starts using the House gym real soon.

PART TWO
THE WEASELS
Truer Words Are Never Spoken. Ever.

4

LYING IN STATE

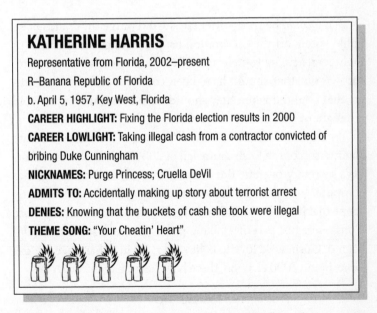

KATHERINE HARRIS

Representative from Florida, 2002–present

R–Banana Republic of Florida

b. April 5, 1957, Key West, Florida

CAREER HIGHLIGHT: Fixing the Florida election results in 2000

CAREER LOWLIGHT: Taking illegal cash from a contractor convicted of bribing Duke Cunningham

NICKNAMES: Purge Princess; Cruella DeVil

ADMITS TO: Accidentally making up story about terrorist arrest

DENIES: Knowing that the buckets of cash she took were illegal

THEME SONG: "Your Cheatin' Heart"

I am a bit biased. I co-chair the campaign effort of George W. Bush. . . . I hope it will be "W."

—KATHERINE HARRIS in 2000

Call her Representative B. That's what prosecutors call Katherine Harris, in the case of defense contractor Mitchell Wade. (Although judging by the ample "running mates" straining at her tight sweaters, it's probably the only time she associated with a "B".) Anyway, Wade pleaded guilty to bribing Duke Cunningham and admitted funneling about thirty-two grand to Katherine, too. But Katherine swears she didn't know she was accepting illegal money, and of course the money had nothing to do with her subsequent attempt to get a ten-million-dollar contract for his company. The government is taking her at her word. And yet we find it awfully difficult to believe anything she says. Start with this claim:

> No partisan activity transpired in my office during the recount period.

That *could* be true—after all, she did purge thousands of eligible voters off the registration list for Voting While Black (or Democrat) *before* the election. But there were all those votes thrown out that should have been counted, and all those others that counted when they should have been thrown out. And what about this claim:

She says she built a "firewall" between her duties as state chairperson of the Bush campaign in 2000 and her duties as Florida's secretary of state. But investigators who went through her computer hard drive to check on that "firewall" found her dreamy "hope that it will be 'W.' " The Purge Princess maintains that those words were just part of a talking-points memo that she never delivered. Gosh, we'd love to believe her; it's just that since her exploits in the 2000 election, there have been so many other lies.

Fantastic Fib

While campaigning for her beloved president in 2004, Harris informed an audience in Florida about a terrorist plot to blow up the power grid of Carmel, Indiana. She said she'd heard about it from the town's mayor, who told her they'd arrested a "Middle Eastern man" with hundreds of pounds of explosives in his home. It was an inspiring story that proved once again that President Bush Is Keeping Us Safer. Except that she made it up. The mayor was questioned by a reporter (who perhaps didn't trust Kathy), and guess what? He never met Katherine, much less told her about a nonexistent plot involving a nonexistent "Middle Eastern man."

Katherine ran for Congress in 2002, and even the official quitting of her job as secretary of state involved dishonesty. State law required her to file a formal letter of resignation, but she claimed she didn't know the law applied to her. Somehow she won that election and then was reelected, proving that she disqualified the wrong voters back in 2000.

Cruella is making headlines—none of them good—running for the Senate against Bill Nelson. The party did everything but take her mascara away to try to stop her, and they mounted an "anybody but Katherine" campaign. (Wow, it must really have stung when the Bush brothers ditched her, after all she did for them.) Yet she maintained that everything was hunky-dory.

Hey, Wait, Where's Everybody Going? Don't Leave Me Here Alone . . .

After the revelations about her (inadvertently) accepting illegal contributions, even her campaign manager told her to drop out of the race, but our brave Kitty flew up to New York, marched herself over to Fox News, and for once wearing slightly less makeup than a female impersonator, announced that she'd spend her own dead daddy's millions, since nobody else would give her money. And then later, campaign aides implied she'd decided not to spend her inheritance after all. And then after that, they pretty much all quit. Really—her cam-

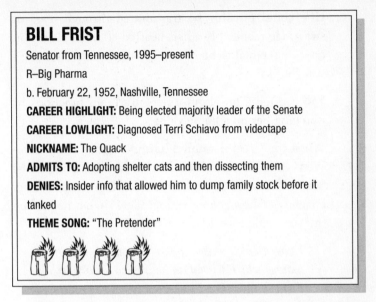

BILL FRIST

Senator from Tennessee, 1995–present

R–Big Pharma

b. February 22, 1952, Nashville, Tennessee

CAREER HIGHLIGHT: Being elected majority leader of the Senate

CAREER LOWLIGHT: Diagnosed Terri Schiavo from videotape

NICKNAME: The Quack

ADMITS TO: Adopting shelter cats and then dissecting them

DENIES: Insider info that allowed him to dump family stock before it tanked

THEME SONG: "The Pretender"

When they make the Bill Frist biopic, it's got to be called *Disgrace Under Pressure.* (Either that or *Silence of the Kitties*, given his med-school penchant for adopting shelter kitties and then dissecting them for "science.")

Any way you look at the life of William Harrison Frist, you come up with a career built on lying, hypocrisy, and crumbling under pressure. If his Hippocratic Oath states "First, do no harm," his Hypocritical Oath is "First, do some pandering."

Lessons Learned at Harvard Med School, by Dr. Bill Frist:

1. **Intelligent design should be taught alongside evolution.** Therefore, we presume that as a cardiothoracic surgeon he can show you just where God reached in and took Adam's rib to make Eve. His position on intelligent design makes him a laughingstock in the reality-based medical community, but when he's hanging with his homies at Justice Sunday rallies, he's got to be able to convince them he's really on their side.

2. **HIV could possibly be transmitted through tears or sweat.** He made only a half-hearted effort to claim this one. He seemed to be having a hard time maintaining a straight face.

3. **You can tell a lot about a person's brain functions by watching her on a home video.**

When the Creator wanted him to diagnose Terri Schiavo via videotape, Dr. Frist had no problem going to the Senate floor and saying she was looking sharp to him. Diagnosis: She's gonna be fine! Here's what he said on the Senate floor on March 17, 2005:

> *I question it based on a review of the video footage which I spent an hour or so looking at last night in my office. She certainly seems to respond to visual stimuli.*

Right. You know, Doc, the Mona Lisa seems to follow you with her eyes, too, but that doesn't mean she can see you.

Later, when an autopsy proved that poor Terri had been blind and brain-dead, Doctor Quack had an easy solution. He lied. He denied having said it. The fact that he said it on television, on videotape, slowed him down a little, as did the outrage from the American public. Remember, Doc, if you're going to pander, you have to know what the people want.

Insider Trading or Just Plain Lucky?

Now, if posturing were illegal, there'd be nobody left in Congress. But insider trading is another story. And while Dr. Quack vehemently denies it, the government is looking into whether or not he'd been tipped off when he dumped some of his family's hospital stock right before its price tanked. He says he didn't even know he owned the stock, HCA, because it was in a blind trust. More like a nearsighted one; he knew at least that he had some HCA stock because he told his broker to sell it. (Sometimes we just want to tap him on the shoulder and say "Hello . . . we can hear you . . .")

On the other hand, maybe he didn't know what was going to happen to the stock. It wouldn't have been the first time he was surprised by events. As majority leader of the Senate, in fact, he seems to be in a nearly perpetual state of shock as his own party deserts him and maneuvers around him as they see fit, and Harry Reid reduces him to whining about parliamentary tricks. His Republican colleagues snickered at his panicky, desperate attempt to soothe voters' rage over gas prices with a half-assed plan to give every American a hundred-dollar rebate check. It was dead on arrival. You'd think a doctor would recognize a DOA, wouldn't you?

Doc, here's some news. Members of your own party think you've been an inept majority leader, and the Christian extremists who wanted to bring Terri Schiavo a Red Bull are *crazy*—but they're not stupid. They see right through you, too. If you really want to be taken seriously by anybody, see if one of your old Harvard med school pals will do a spine transplant for you.

CONDOLEEZZA RICE

Secretary of State, 2005–present

b. November 14, 1954, Birmingham, Alabama

CAREER HIGHLIGHT: Being named Secretary of State

CAREER LOWLIGHT: Being spotted buying shoes in fancy store during Katrina crisis

NICKNAMES: Condi; Ferragamo

ADMITS TO: Wanting to be NFL Commissioner

DENIES: Being a liar

THEME SONG: "Wishin' and Hopin'"

Scene: Nighttime, interior, Watergate apartment, Washington, D.C. A half-empty bottle of red wine rests on a coaster embossed with the presidential seal. Glenn Gould music is playing softly in the background. A tall, attractive African American woman stands in front of a mirror over a Louis XIV writing table. On the table is a photograph of George and Laura Bush, which is signed, "To our Condi, with warmest affection, GWB." Mrs. Bush's face appears to have been gouged out with a paper clip.

The woman speaks to her reflection in the mirror: "I don't know how much longer I can go on lying for him. Daddy was right—I have to think about my future. He'll never leave her. And he'll be retired in a couple of years, and then what am I supposed to do? Besides, he doesn't even know when I'm telling the truth and when I'm lying to cover for him. I'm so confused." *She lifts the wineglass to her lips and swallows the last drops, then walks over for a refill.*

Okay, enough of the fantasy sequence. We'd like to believe that Condi Rice lies for love. Hey, who hasn't been there once or twice? And she was once reported to have slipped and referred to the president as "my husb—the president" at a Washington party. But after careful review, it appears she lies to cover her ass, the president's ass, Dick Cheney's ass (eeew), and the whole sorry lot of them.

Remember, Condoleezza Rice was national security adviser in the first Bush term; that means she was in charge of our *national security*. So when she was caught on September 11, 2001, doing a lousy job at keeping us secure, it was time to open a giant economy-size can of CYA. And as you can see, as each lie was told and then debunked, another lie was told to cover the one before. But it began with the mother of all lies:

> *I don't think anybody could have predicted that they would try to use an airplane as a missile, a hijacked airplane as a missile.*
>
> —CONDOLEEZZA RICE, May 16, 2002

Of course, we know now that somebody could have predicted just that—because somebody did. Lots of somebodies. For one, the infamous August 6, 2001, Presidential Daily Brief that was entitled "Bin Laden Determined to Strike in the U.S." warned that the FBI had picked up al-Qaeda activity "consistent with preparations for hijackings." (You know, the "historical document," as she first called it, was only a page and a half long—couldn't somebody have read it, even on vacation?)

When that lie was discovered, she covered it by saying that the president, in fact, had requested the briefing because he was so worried about the elevated terrorist threats that summer. Impressive, but untrue. The 9/11 panel says that the author of the briefing doesn't recall a request coming from the president and that the idea came from within the CIA.

Oops. But that PDB thing was just a tragic lapse in an otherwise rock-solid national security machine, right?

In June and July when the threat spikes were so high . . . we were at battle stations.

—CONDOLEEZZA RICE, March 22, 2004

Well, if by battle stations you mean driving golf balls and clearing brush at the Crawford faux ranch, maybe. According to *The Washington Post*, on August 9, 2001, Attorney General John Ashcroft's "strategic plan" didn't list fighting terrorism as one of the Justice Department's top seven goals. And the administration was planning to end a classified program to monitor the whereabouts of al-Qaeda suspects. By the way, it wasn't as if the FAA wasn't warned—they just failed to act appropriately.

According to a report from the 9/11 commission, the FAA received fifty-two warnings that mentioned Bin Laden or al-Qaeda between April and September 10, and five of them specifically warned about hijackings. You'll be surprised to learn that the Bush administration tried to block the release of that report, knowing (we assume) that it would require further ass-covering. The full report still isn't out.

Condi also stated that "the fact of the matter is that the administration focused on this before 9/11." And yet the vice president's counterterrorism task force never met, not once.

When it came to the Iraq war, Condi was more of a multinational liar, lying about when the decision was made to go to war against Iraq (apparently, while the president was still reading "The Pet Goat" in Florida, Rummy was trying to pull together a war plan). She said they didn't know there were doubts about the intelligence the president and Colin Powell used to make their case for war . . . but that's not true, either. There were warnings from the CIA, we now know. And of course there was her claim that if we didn't attack Saddam, the smoking gun could turn into "a mushroom cloud."

There are more, many more, examples, and if you want to give yourself a migraine you may want to check out some of the political blogs, like americanprogress.org, that make it their business to keep track of Condi's dishonesty.

Why, Condi, why? Do you love your job that much? Does Dick Cheney crawl out of his undisclosed location and threaten you with a shotgun? Is it your husb—the president? You're so smart, and you look so hot in those CFM boots (Did you buy them in New York while people were dying in New Orleans, by the way? Just asking), that it's too bad your integrity is part of the collateral damage of the Bush administration.

It was great to see you try a little honesty on for size in England, when you said the United States had made "thousands" of mistakes in Iraq, even if you did take it back the very next day by saying you were only speaking figuratively.

Too bad about all the unpleasant booing and protesting in Britain. It's a shame Paul McCartney declined your invitation to meet in Liverpool, although we're sure it was almost as exciting to visit a school he once attended there. And too bad about all those antiwar protesters shouting about the blood on your hands. We're beginning to think you mean it when you say you don't want to run for president.

Classics from the Republican Reading Room

Republicans have so many talents, but as we've seen in the last few years, they are most gifted at storytelling. No surprise, then, that so many of them are novelists. If you're going to be telling tall tales, why not get paid to do it? Take the accused perjurer Lewis "Scooter" Libby. He's a guy who's had some trouble keeping his nose clean—maybe because he spent a lot of time with it stuck in the soft-core porno passages of his debut novel, *The Apprentice*. We don't know whether he told the truth to the grand jury about the Valerie Plame affair, but he certainly has a colorful way with words.

WARNING: NOT APPROPRIATE FOR CHILDREN.

THE APPRENTICE
by Scooter Libby

*T*HE YOUNG SAMURAI'S MOTHER HAD THE CHILD
sold to a brothel, where she swept the floors and
oiled the women and watched the secret ways. At age ten
the madam put the child in a cage with a bear trained to
couple with young girls so the girls would be frigid and not
fall in love with their patrons. They fed her through the
bars and aroused the bear with a stick when it seemed to
lose interest. Groups of men paid to watch. Like other
girls who have been trained this way, she learned to handle many men in a single night and her skin turned a
milky white.

Stories of this north-country training for prostitutes
were apparently well known among the guests, who made
impatient motions for Ueda to continue . . . "Then," Ueda
said, "they trained the young whore in all of the finest
ways to pleasure men. They gave her wooden penises and
taught her how to handle them. They taught her how to
sing out in the night and move to finish off her customers
more quickly. . . ."

"They taught her how to draw pubic hair on her
mound," Ueda laughed, "because she was still too young
to have any of her own."

We can only pray that someone gave Phyllis Schlafly
and James Dobson their very own copies of Scooter's
book.

5

FAMILY VALUES DOESN'T MEAN VALUING FAMILIES
Governmental Affairs Committee

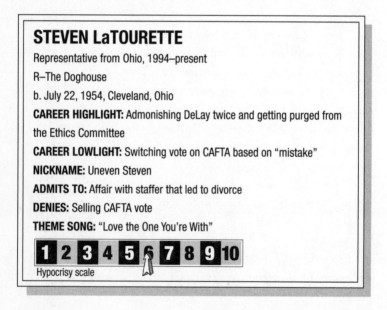

STEVEN LaTOURETTE

Representative from Ohio, 1994–present

R–The Doghouse

b. July 22, 1954, Cleveland, Ohio

CAREER HIGHLIGHT: Admonishing DeLay twice and getting purged from the Ethics Committee

CAREER LOWLIGHT: Switching vote on CAFTA based on "mistake"

NICKNAME: Uneven Steven

ADMITS TO: Affair with staffer that led to divorce

DENIES: Selling CAFTA vote

THEME SONG: "Love the One You're With"

1 2 **3** 4 **5** 6 **7** 8 **9** 10

Hypocrisy scale

Congressmen are gods. Senators are gods. And there are tons of aides and tons of lobbyists, and they kiss their butts and they love

that. Power corrupts, and I think the longer you're there, the more corrupt you become.

—SUSAN LATOURETTE, ex-wife

"Bitter . . . table for one." Who can blame Susan LaTourette, ex-wife of Congressman Steve LaTourette, for being bitter? Wouldn't you be if your husband of twenty-one years, the father of your children, called from D.C. one day to say he had a girlfriend and wanted a divorce? But this is not just a story of Desperate Ex-Housewives and their straying husbands.

No, this LaTourette's syndrome is a tale of moral hypocrisy, spotty ethics, and stupidity. A Naked Republicans trifecta!

Steve was first elected to Congress in 1994, and fell in line as one of the spawn of Gingrich. His strategy seemed to be to stay under the radar and try not to piss off either his new right-wing masters or his moderate constituents back home. One constituent he did piss off back home was his wife, but we're getting ahead of ourselves.

Steve had a solid "family values" voting record, and was a good soldier for the Christian Coalition. Of course, that meant he was shocked and outraged at Bill Clinton's behavior, and yes, he did vote to impeach him. Which is why, when he called home a few years later to tell his wife he was having an affair with a former staffer and wanted a divorce, he earned his tarnished halo in Hypocrite Heaven.

His wife, Susan, on the other hand, earned a medal from the Hell Hath No Fury Club. Not only did she go to the press to complain about her soon-to-be-ex, but she placed campaign signs for his opponent on the front lawn of their home during the 2004 campaign.

But what about the new Mrs. LaTourette? Funny story—if the appearance of corruption makes you laugh. The aptly named Jennifer Laptook, Steve's former chief of staff, left his office to become a lobbyist. Now the meager ethics rules that do exist say you can't lobby your former boss for at least a year. But Jennifer has landed some nice paydays while lobbying the House Transportation and Infrastructure Committee that Steve sits on. See, she's not lobbying him, it's just his committee. So that makes it okay, or at least, not technically against the rules. (Steve knows the rules well—he also sat on the ethics committee and even voted to slap Tom DeLay's wrists a couple of times before he got purged for his efforts.)

While we're on the subject of screwing, that's what Steve did to his constituents when he broke his promise to vote against the CAFTA treaty. A simple misunderstanding, he said.

The Cleveland *Plain Dealer* put it like this:

LaTourette Attributes Flip-Flop on CAFTA to Tariff No One Pays

Ohio, you must be very proud.

SUE MYRICK

Representative from North Carolina, 1994–present

R–Amway

b. August 1, 1941, Tiffin, Ohio

CAREER HIGHLIGHT: Reelected mayor after hammering Democrat for using pot and coke in the '70s

CAREER LOWLIGHT: Forced to admit she had an affair in the '70s

MARITAL STATUS: Married

NICKNAME: Saint Sue

ADMITS TO: Fear of swarthy convenience store clerks

DENIES: Anti-Arab remark about convenience stores

THEME SONG: "Whip It"

1 2 3 4 5 6 7 8 9 10
Hypocrisy scale

As sad as this is for our nation, this action is necessary so that all of us can continue to not only uphold but teach those basic truths and basic right and wrong in our houses and most assuredly in this House. . . . Yes, we need to confess and repair and repent. Just remember, the children are watching.

—SUE MYRICK

And so it was with a heavy heart that Sue Myrick cast her vote to impeach Bill Clinton. Sue knew a lot about confession and repenting—you see, she had already confessed to an affair with a married man when she was running for reelection as mayor of Charlotte in 1989. It was a tough time for her—she even cursed at a caller during a radio phone-in show, and had to apologize for that, too.

She doesn't always apologize for her poor choice of words. There was the time she was giving a little talk about domestic terror when she shared her secret fear of Arabs by accidentally saying this out loud:

> *You know, and this can be misconstrued, but honest to goodness, Ed [husband] and I, for years, for twenty years, have been saying, "You know, look at who runs all the convenience stores across the country. Every little town you go into, you know?"*

Later she clarified her comments by saying "I've got Arab friends." And before you say, "Oh, no, she didn't"—let us say, oh, yes, she did.

But Sue doesn't like to dwell on unpleasant or controversial things, like the fact that she used to make her living as an Amway distributor, and that Amway members have contributed generously to her campaigns. You won't see the word "Amway" anywhere on her official website biography, although she did host a lavish fundraiser for Rick Lazio on the Amway yacht when he was running for the Senate against Hillary Clinton.

It Takes "God-Sized Strength" to Be Sue Myrick

Like all of the best Amway salespeople, Sue is a hard-driving, ambitious gal, and it pays off in her committee assignments. She was chair of the important Republican Study Committee, a cabal of conservatives who meet regularly to figure out which corporations to do favors for and which civil liberties to curtail. And how did she find the strength and wisdom to be such a powerful leader? If you're guessing it came from Jesus, well, you've been invited to the right luncheons (or at least you've been reading *Roll Call*). We didn't realize that it takes "God-sized strength to be a member of the powerful Rules Committee," but if you got invited to lunch with Sue and the Center for Christian Statesmanship, you were only too aware that "Representative Myrick fights spiritual battles as she helps others learn how to rely on Christ."

We're sure Saint Sue has had her hands full with the spiritual battles going on in Congress these days. We're not saying she's part of the culture of corruption, mind you, but we can't help but notice that she spent the last two years in Tom DeLay's pocket.

- She voted with DeLay more than 90 percent of the time.

- She voted to weaken the Ethics Committee rules to protect him.

- And, as she must have learned on her Amway training tapes, she didn't walk away without some of his cash—a few thousand dollars from his ARMPAC fund.

In case you're wondering: Yes, she got a few bucks from an Abramoff client, too. For reasons known perhaps only to Sue and Jack, she signed a letter urging the Bush administration to reject a Louisiana tribe's application for a casino.

By the end of 2005, Sue had probably had enough of probing questions from reporters. Besides Abramoff and DeLay, she had to answer some tough questions about her claim that three al-Qaeda members had been caught near the Mexican border. She said it at a news conference where she was proposing tough new legislation to fight illegal immigration. But when reporters questioned her, she was forced to admit it never happened. She got her facts wrong from a year-old story in *Time* magazine, her people said. Maybe she found it at a convenience store run by Arabs.

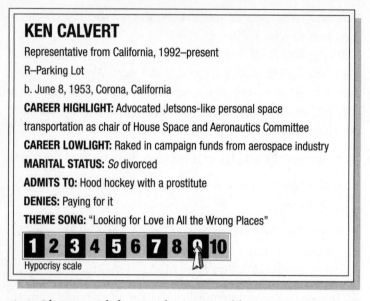

KEN CALVERT

Representative from California, 1992–present

R–Parking Lot

b. June 8, 1953, Corona, California

CAREER HIGHLIGHT: Advocated Jetsons-like personal space transportation as chair of House Space and Aeronautics Committee

CAREER LOWLIGHT: Raked in campaign funds from aerospace industry

MARITAL STATUS: *So* divorced

ADMITS TO: Hood hockey with a prostitute

DENIES: Paying for it

THEME SONG: "Looking for Love in All the Wrong Places"

1 2 3 4 5 6 7 8 9 10
Hypocrisy scale

As a Christian, I believe in the concept of forgiveness. We can forgive the actions. We can't forget what occurred.

—KEN CALVERT, in the Riverside *Press-Enterprise*,
September 11, 1998

Thus did Congressman Calvert display the kind of Christian values that have earned him a 100 percent rating from the Family Research Council for his voting record in Congress. He was referring, of course, to President Clinton and his Monica Lewinsky situation. And good old Ken was just the guy to advise the President about what to do when you get caught with your pants down—literally. He had been there and done that.

It was November 28, 1993, and Ken had been representing the good people of Southern California's Forty-fourth District for less than a year. Police officers from Corona drove past a parked car and apparently interrupted Ken as he was engaged in (receiving?) a sex act from a local hooker. Ken, just like Bill Clinton, denied having sexual relations with that woman (Miss

Lewin—er, Miss Linberg, known to police as a prostitute and heroin user). Initially the police said they saw the congressman in his car but didn't actually see any criminal activity, so they let him leave. The Riverside *Press-Enterprise* was skeptical, though, and they went to court to force the Corona police to release their report. Here are some of the details from the police report, as quoted by the Riverside *Press-Enterprise*:

> *I noticed that the male subject was placing his penis into his unzipped dress slacks, and was trying to hide it with his untucked dress shirt . . . the male subject started his vehicle and . . . proceeded to leave. I ordered him three times to turn off the vehicle and he finally stopped and complied. . . . The male identified himself as Kenneth Stanton Calvert . . . and stated "We're just talking, that's all, nothing else." . . . I spoke with [Calvert's female companion, Lore Lorena] Linberg separately. I asked her if she had ever been arrested for anything, and she said, "Yes, for prostitution and under the influence of heroin." Linberg said she had last "shot up" approximately one week prior and is currently on methadone.*

Once the ugly facts were published, Ken quickly apologized, and then made the rather implausible assertion that he had not paid for sex from a working girl. (Somehow we doubt she did it for a slim volume of *Leaves of Grass*.)

Eventually Calvert explained his conduct: "I was feeling intensely lonely." He did not, however, offer any explanation of why he had lied about having oral sex with a woman who was not his wife. Hey, wait . . . isn't lying about sex why you voted to impeach Clinton, Ken?

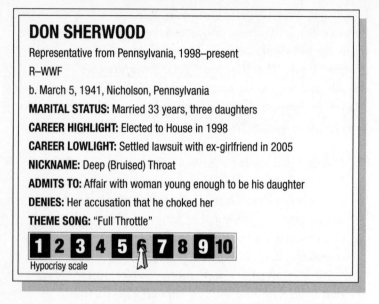

DON SHERWOOD

Representative from Pennsylvania, 1998–present

R–WWF

b. March 5, 1941, Nicholson, Pennsylvania

MARITAL STATUS: Married 33 years, three daughters

CAREER HIGHLIGHT: Elected to House in 1998

CAREER LOWLIGHT: Settled lawsuit with ex-girlfriend in 2005

NICKNAME: Deep (Bruised) Throat

ADMITS TO: Affair with woman young enough to be his daughter

DENIES: Her accusation that he choked her

THEME SONG: "Full Throttle"

1 2 3 4 5 6 7 8 9 10

Hypocrisy scale

No Happy Ending for This Massage

He's just not that into you. Girls, we've all been there. You fall in love with an older guy, maybe one old enough to be your father, because he makes you feel safe, and, frankly, hot. You convince yourself he's really going to get a divorce. Or maybe you know deep in your heart he won't, but you're having fun. Everything is going along just fine, and then one day, blammo, out of nowhere, the nice affair turns into a big box of wrong. The next thing you know you're half naked, locked in the bathroom calling 911. Sound familiar? No?

Congressman Don Sherwood got to Washington in 1999, just a few weeks too late to impeach Bill Clinton. But it was clear that this family man and former car dealer had his work cut out for him. Washington was obviously a cesspool of immorality, of loose women and predatory men. He must have known he would fit right in . . . joining the pantheon of horny middle-aged Republicans led by the recently disgraced Bob Livingston, Henry "youthful indiscretion" Hyde, and the former speaker, Newt Gingrich.

Did Big Don have cheating on his mind when he went to a gathering of Young Republicans later that first year? Apparently, that's where he met young Cynthia Ore. Their affair must have begun fairly soon after that, because he's admitted to having a five-year affair with her and we can do the math.

Did the affair start before or after he voted to allow the posting of the Ten Commandments in public schools, including, we believe, that one about adultery? And you know what happens to adulterers, don't you? Open your Bibles to Leviticus, everybody:

> *And the man that committeth adultery with another man's wife, even he that committeth adultery with his neighbor's wife, the adulterer and the adulteress shall surely be put to death.*
>
> —Leviticus 20:10

That seems way harsh, we know, but luckily, while he was a married man, Cynthia was a single woman, so no need to putteth anybody to death. She told the Wilkes-Barre *Times Leader* that when they met, he told her he was getting a divorce.

As the relationship went on, Don was busy establishing his credentials with the family values crowd. Knowing from personal experience that marriage needs a lot of defending, he voted for the Defense of Marriage Act. He also went for the constitutional amendment to ban gay marriage (and threw in an anti-gay adoption vote, too, just for good measure).

And for his work he got a 100 percent approval rating from Donald Wildmon's American Family Association. What's their mission?

The American Family Association exists to motivate and equip citizens to change the culture to reflect Biblical truth.

—AFA MISSION STATEMENT

Biblical truth is one thing (although we're not exactly sure what)—but telling the truth to the cops is something else. In the fall of 2004, Cynthia called 911 from the bathroom of Don's Capitol Hill apartment to report that he'd assaulted her. At first when the cops came, Don insisted he barely knew her, but he acknowledged that he had been giving this woman a massage when she inexplicably jumped up and ran into the bathroom. Eventually he came clean (as it were) and admitted to having had a five-year affair with her. But he maintained he never hit her or choked her. Still, it does invite the question, If you didn't assault her, why settle out of court when she sued you for five million bucks? We'll never know, since the settlement is confidential. Clearly, though, this was one massage that didn't conclude with a "happy ending."

Don's being taken care of by his friends in the Republican leadership. (Voting with his fallen leader Tom DeLay 95 percent of the time has to be good for something, after all.) Denny Hastert, Roy Blunt, and a bunch of the other guys and gals have all sent PAC money his way. You know how friends will pass the hat for a buddy who's fallen on hard financial times through no fault of his own. We especially like the fact that some of the money is from a fund called the Retain Our Majority Program, or ROMP. Seems extra appropriate for Donny!

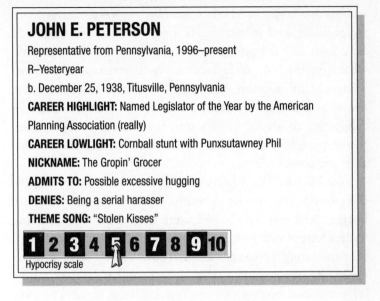

JOHN E. PETERSON

Representative from Pennsylvania, 1996–present

R–Yesteryear

b. December 25, 1938, Titusville, Pennsylvania

CAREER HIGHLIGHT: Named Legislator of the Year by the American Planning Association (really)

CAREER LOWLIGHT: Cornball stunt with Punxsutawney Phil

NICKNAME: The Gropin' Grocer

ADMITS TO: Possible excessive hugging

DENIES: Being a serial harasser

THEME SONG: "Stolen Kisses"

1 2 3 4 5 6 7 8 9 10

Hypocrisy scale

Why sugarcoat what everyone knows to be true? The emperor has no clothes.

—JOHN PETERSON, about President Clinton,
May 1998

It may well be that old John Peterson knows firsthand just how the emperor felt. He was a small-town grocer running for Congress in 1996 as a conservative determined to restore integrity to Washington. But in the heat of the campaign, he was accused of putting the "gross" in "grocer."

A group of women from the state government came forward to accuse him of copping feels whenever the spirit moved him. Three women accused him of forcibly kissing them, and three others said he made them feel uncomfortable and asked to be transferred out of his office. And one woman said he grabbed her breast in an elevator when she was a teenage Senate page. Because it was always a matter of he said/she said, only John and the young women in his path know for sure what happened. We do know that while Peterson was wagging a finger at Bill Clinton, a whole lot of women were fingering *him* as a serial groper. And when the Pennsylvania state senate conducted an official inquiry into the charges of the former Senate page, they concluded that the incident had "most probably" occurred.

For his part, Big John denied all the charges, although he did concede that maybe he was guilty of being an "excessive hugger." And just for good measure he had his wife Saundra write a letter to the public saying he was the "most honest, decent and caring" person she knew. (Poor woman—somehow we doubt she was rewarded, Mrs. Kobe Bryant style, with a big, juicy diamond in return for eating humiliation for him.) As for Big John, he blamed his opponent for spreading the story. It worked. He went to the House in 1996 and began what can only be fairly described as a lackluster career representing western Pennsylvania.

When he wasn't railing against the dishonesty and loose morals of the president, the good congressman was slavishly following the agenda of the House leadership. Still, he found himself in the embarrassing position of having to defend a hundred-thousand-dollar slab of pork he'd slipped into the bloated federal budget for a weather museum in Punxsutawney, Pa., home of Punxsutawney Phil, the groundhog of Groundhog Day fame. After being accused of wasting tax dollars with an idiotic and unnecessary project, Big John actually brought Phil to Washington to use as a rodent shield against harsh criticism at a news conference.

We can't be sure *who* Big John would like to be drilling, but we know *where*. Late in 2005, he sponsored a bill that would have allowed offshore drilling for natural gas; thankfully, it was roundly defeated.

As for the accusations that he was a Schwarzenegger-in-training during his groping years in the Pennsylvania legislature, John said it best at the time: "It can haunt me forever. It's definitely a political noose around my neck."

6

ASK WHAT YOUR COUNTRY CAN DO FOR YOU

Hold Tight to Your Dreams (and Your Wallet)

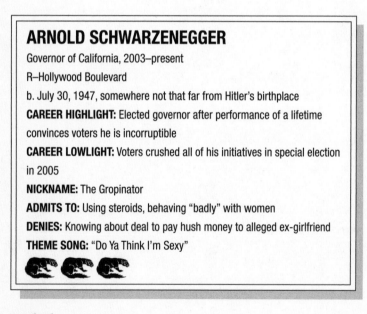

ARNOLD SCHWARZENEGGER

Governor of California, 2003–present

R–Hollywood Boulevard

b. July 30, 1947, somewhere not that far from Hitler's birthplace

CAREER HIGHLIGHT: Elected governor after performance of a lifetime convinces voters he is incorruptible

CAREER LOWLIGHT: Voters crushed all of his initiatives in special election in 2005

NICKNAME: The Gropinator

ADMITS TO: Using steroids, behaving "badly" with women

DENIES: Knowing about deal to pay hush money to alleged ex-girlfriend

THEME SONG: "Do Ya Think I'm Sexy"

We had outercourse.

—GIGI GOYETTE, referring to her relationship with Arnold

You have to hand it to Arnold. Even when it comes to something as old hat as a guy cheating on his wife, Arnold is an innovator—he has to have "outercourse." You could say Arnold puts a new twist on all kinds of old games.

Take Gigi Goyette. The big scandal wasn't that they had some kind of weird sexual relationship that began when she was a teenager. The scandal was about the money she was paid to keep her mouth shut. Turns out that right after Arnold announced his candidacy for governor, American Media, which publishers *The National Enquirer* and some other tabloids, paid Gigi twenty thousand dollars for her story. The deal was she couldn't talk about it to anybody else. When they didn't publish it, it began to seem a lot like hush money, and she eventually told the story to a reporter.

Arnold Gets Muscled Out of "Supplemental Income"—Literally

Of course, it would just be a sexcapade cover-up if there weren't a nasty conflict of interest buried in the deal. Several months later, Arnold joined the American Media payroll, to the tune of millions of dollars, to act as editor of some of their muscle magazines. Political observers thought it was an odd thing, to say the least, for him to be making that kind of outside money while he was serving as governor, and he agreed to donate his "editor's" salary to charity.

But what he didn't reveal was that he still stood to earn millions from the sale of supplements advertised in the magazines. And when a bill to limit the sale of supplements to school kids came to Arnold's desk, he vetoed it. When critics again howled that it was a clear conflict of interest, Arnold finally cut his ties with American Media.

Unfortunately, it was just one of a long trail of weasel deals and conflicts that have helped cause his approval ratings to plummet. For a guy who campaigned on the slogan that he was too rich to buy off, he sure looks like he's for sale:

- On the same day that he vetoed a bill that the insurance industry opposed, he got a check for $105,000 from the American Insurance Association. Probably just a coincidence.

- The same day that one of the owners of Wal-Mart gave his special election campaign $250,000, he vetoed a bill Wal-Mart hated. Just lucky timing on that one, too.

- The agriculture industry was not feeling the love from Arnold. Farmers complained to him that they were getting hammered by regulations and fees. But that was before the growers contributed nearly two million dollars to Arnold's campaign coffers. Suddenly, almost all those onerous bills got vetoed.

- Arnold promised he wouldn't take contributions from companies that do business with the State of California. But he must have forgotten that promise when he did a twenty-million-dollar deal with Enterprise Rent-A-Car after Enterprise gave him a fat campaign contribution. Okay, so maybe he wasn't for sale. Maybe he was just for rent.

None of the money he "raised" was for himself, mind you. It was all for the good of the state. 2005 was supposed to be the year of reform for California, and Arnold spent something like fifty million dollars of taxpayer money to hold a special election so that voters could pass his four ballot propositions.

Election day was the low point of his political career, at least so far. The voters, pissed off at his bullying tactics with the state legislature and public service unions, voted down every single one of his bright ideas.

Hey, nice going, California. Way to pick a governor. Next time, maybe go with Gary Coleman or one of the dozens of other better qualified candidates who ran against Arnold in the recall.

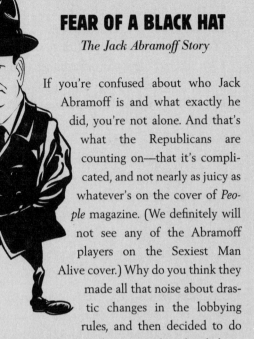

FEAR OF A BLACK HAT
The Jack Abramoff Story

If you're confused about who Jack Abramoff is and what exactly he did, you're not alone. And that's what the Republicans are counting on—that it's complicated, and not nearly as juicy as whatever's on the cover of *People* magazine. (We definitely will not see any of the Abramoff players on the Sexiest Man Alive cover.) Why do you think they made all that noise about drastic changes in the lobbying rules, and then decided to do practically nothing to clean up their act? They decided nobody gets it, or cares. But it's not so hard. Remember these three killer *B*'s: Bilking, Bribing, and Bullshitting.

Sure, prosecutors use terms like "fraud" and "conspiracy," but they'd use the three *B*'s if they could.

MEET THE F**KERS

Who is this Abramoff guy, besides being one of the most notorious sleazebags to hit Washington in a generation?

Jack Abramoff, 47, was probably just another nice Jewish boy at Brandeis University in the 1980s until he fell in with the wrong crowd—the College Republicans. As its chairman, he got to know conservative gangstas-in-training like Grover Norquist and then Karl Rove.

He became a lobbyist in Washington in 1994 at a law firm where he met future partner and co-felon Michael Scanlon and Christian Coalition chief Ralph Reed, among others. The Northern Mariana Islands were a client, and over the years he arranged dozens of lavish trips for members of Congress. In exchange, he wanted help on favorable labor and tax regulations for the garment industry there. Tom DeLay's memorable toast to his "dear friend Jack" came during one of those trips. Jack stayed at that firm until 2001, when he was enticed to go to work for a firm called Greenberg Traurig, where he began to represent Indian tribes with casinos. That's when things got crazy.

MICHAEL SCANLON: Co-weasel to Jack Abramoff. Former press secretary to Tom DeLay. Opened a PR firm to which his friend Jack sent clients. Unbeknownst to them, Scanlon was kicking back part of their exorbitant fees to Jack.

ADAM KIDAN: Despite Congressman Bob Ney's glowing words about him in the *Congressional Record*, he was a crook who partnered with Jack on a phony cruise ship deal in Miami.

THE CHARGES: Keep in mind that there were two different prosecutions going against Jack, one with Scanlon, one with Kidan.

Let's start with the Bilking and Bribing: This is the Washington case in which Abramoff admitted to corruption charges.

"SERGEANT" BILKO

Abramoff bilked Indian tribe clients out of millions of dollars—they paid him and his secret partner Michael Scanlon about eighty million dollars between 2000 and 2003. Some of Abramoff's money came in the form of secret kickbacks from Scanlon. Did we mention that he referred to his clients in e-mails as "monkeys," "idiots," and "troglodytes"? (He's sorry, he says.)

Scanlon also pleaded guilty and is cooperating with prosecutors. He ran a public relations company called Capitol Campaign Strategies whose client list was full of Abramoff referrals. In what may be the most egregious scheme of all, Abramoff and Scanlon worked to get the Tigua tribe's Texas casino closed in 2002, and then went to the Tiguas offering to help get the casino reopened for the small fee of $4.2 million. The Tiguas paid . . . but the casino never did reopen.

HERE COME THE BRIBES

Abramoff had two restaurants, skyboxes at Washington area sports venues, and lots and lots and *lots* of money to win friends and influence congressmen. He says he gave many members of Congress money and free food, entertainment, and travel, in exchange for their help on legislation favorable to his clients. Where it gets sticky is that last part, because pretty much everybody who took his money said he had no influence over them.

The political watchdog group Center for Responsive Politics says that Jack and his various clients contributed more than three and a half million dollars to members of Congress from 2000 to 2006.

THE SHAKEDOWN CRUZ—BULLSHIT AND BILKING

In the Miami case, Jack and Adam Kidan pleaded guilty to fraud and conspiracy charges in a *Producers*-like scheme to buy some gambling yachts in 2000. They admitted to cooking up a fake wire transfer to make it appear that they had anted up twenty-three million dollars to buy SunCruz casinos (the Florida yacht company). By 2004 the company was bankrupt and they were being sued by creditors. Oh, and the guy who sold them the company was found dead in an apparent mob rubout.

If you want all the gory details, check out "The House That Jack Built" at thinkprogress.org and "The Abramoff Primer" by Geov Parrish at workingforchange.com.

Or just wait for your favorite Republican to show up on an episode of *Cops*. Can't you just picture Bob Ney running out of a house trailer in a wifebeater shirt and flip-flops?

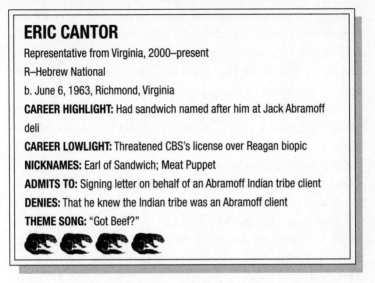

ERIC CANTOR

Representative from Virginia, 2000–present

R–Hebrew National

b. June 6, 1963, Richmond, Virginia

CAREER HIGHLIGHT: Had sandwich named after him at Jack Abramoff deli

CAREER LOWLIGHT: Threatened CBS's license over Reagan biopic

NICKNAMES: Earl of Sandwich; Meat Puppet

ADMITS TO: Signing letter on behalf of an Abramoff Indian tribe client

DENIES: That he knew the Indian tribe was an Abramoff client

THEME SONG: "Got Beef?"

Something Ain't Kosher at Abramoff's Deli

In America, any boy or girl can grow up to be elected to the House of Representatives. But it just may be that only Eric Cantor can have a sandwich named after him at Jack Abramoff's deli.

Let's face it, it must be tough being the only Jewish guy in the room when House Republicans get together. You have to listen to endless stupid cracks from Southern yahoos about bringing home the pork to your district. And you always suspect the wingnuts who are extra nice to you are just hoping you'll hook them up with primo real estate in Jerusalem when it's go-time for the Rapture.

On the other hand, the party leaders are thrilled to have any ethnic group represented, even a Jew who went to a Protestant private school. Sure, when he got to the House, he was kind of an overachiever in that Jewish-kid-from-high-school way, but in no time at all he was in with the in crowd, as the deputy whip. No wonder he caught Jack Abramoff's eye.

Eric would like everybody to remember that he is the one Republican whom Jack Abramoff spent money to *defeat*. Yeah, that's right. Of course, Eric doesn't mention that when he won that election in 2000, Black Jack became a big supporter, to the tune of thousands of dollars. And one infamous sandwich.

You see, Abramoff, regarded as a disgrace by fellow Jews around the world, owned a kosher deli called Stacks. He decided to throw a fundraiser for Eric—a "sandwich naming" party. According to the weekly *Forward* newspaper, the sandwich was originally going to be made of tuna, but Eric wanted something red-meatier, like red meat.

Voilà, we give you "The Eric Cantor." Roast beef on challah bread. Very lean, no doubt. All of this would be only an embarrassment to Eric and to Jews everywhere, were it not for the Abramoff connection. He just might have wanted more from Eric than permission to add a side of coleslaw to his sandwich platter.

Six months after the sandwich caper, Eric signed a letter to Interior Secretary Gale Norton that recommended she reject a tribal casino application. The letter was requested by—you guessed it—Jack Abramoff, who was trying to avoid competition for one of his tribal clients.

We know what you're thinking, but the letter had *absolutely nothing* to do with the thousands of dollars that Abramoff and his clients gave to Cantor. The Earl of Sandwich's office says he was just thinking of interests back home. And he said he didn't even know Abramoff was involved in any way with that letter. He told his hometown paper, the *Richmond Times-Dispatch*, that he knew Abramoff only on a very casual, infrequent basis. Nonetheless, he's returned the Abramoff money.

Hey, bubeleh, here's a serving suggestion. Next time someone names a meal after you, hold the roast beef and go with the weasel.

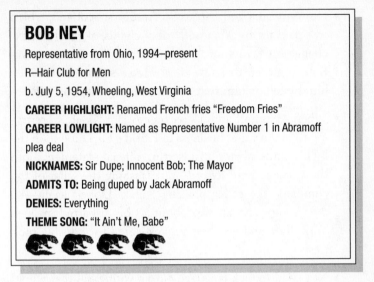

BOB NEY

Representative from Ohio, 1994–present

R–Hair Club for Men

b. July 5, 1954, Wheeling, West Virginia

CAREER HIGHLIGHT: Renamed French fries "Freedom Fries"

CAREER LOWLIGHT: Named as Representative Number 1 in Abramoff plea deal

NICKNAMES: Sir Dupe; Innocent Bob; The Mayor

ADMITS TO: Being duped by Jack Abramoff

DENIES: Everything

THEME SONG: "It Ain't Me, Babe"

Just met with Ney!!! We're f'ing gold!!!! He's going to do Tigua.
            —JACK ABRAMOFF, in a March 20, 2002, e-mail

Some people call Bob Ney the Mayor of Capitol Hill. Federal prosecutors call him "Representative Number 1" in the Abramoff plea agreement. But you can call him Innocent Bob, because all the nasty accusations against him are *just not true.* Except the one about him being the idiot who renamed French fries "Freedom Fries" in the House cafeterias. And French toast was renamed, yes, Freedom Toast. "A small but symbolic gesture," Monsieur Bob called it. *Très stupide,* you might also call it.

Bob Ney was nicknamed "the Mayor" because as chairman of the House Administration Committee, he was the go-to guy for everything from parking spots to office furniture in the Capitol. Unfortunately for Bob, Black Jack Abramoff also thought of him as the go-to guy when he needed to buy some juice in Congress.

The charges that Bob is unjustly accused of include:

- He went on a golf trip to St. Andrews, Scotland, which was paid for by Abramoff tribal clients, allegedly in exchange for favors for Abramoff's buddies. But how was Bob supposed to know that? He says Abramoff duped him by telling him that a nonprofit organization paid.

- When Abramoff and his partner, Adam Kidan, were trying to buy a yacht business in Florida, Sir Dupe took the highly unusual step of inserting official statements into the *Congressional Record*—one trashing the seller of the company, the other praising Kidan. Duped again—he didn't know Kidan was about to be disbarred in New York State and was being investigated for possible mob ties.

- Ney tried to tack language onto a voting bill that would have reopened a casino for Abramoff's client, the Tigua tribe. He was foiled in the Senate by Chris Dodd of Connecticut, who rejected the Tigua Indian stuff. You'll never guess what happened there—Ney says he was duped by Abramoff on that one, too. Kind of a gullible dude, ain't he?

- Shortly after Ney agreed to "do Tigua," as Abramoff put it in his e-mail to colleague Michael Scanlon (a former top DeLay aide), Abramoff asked the Tigua tribe's political consultant to send checks totaling thirty-two thousand dollars to Sir Dupe. "F'ing gold" indeed.

Those are just *some* of the highlights in the list of allegations. But not all of Innocent Bob's problems were caused by Jack Abramoff. Sometimes it's someone else's fault.

In February 2003, Bob and an aide were flown to London by a guy named Nigel Winfield, who wanted to sell American-made airplane parts to Iran. He wanted Bob to get the sanctions against Iran lifted. What Bob didn't know was that Mr.

Winfield was a three-time loser who'd been to jail for an earlier scam to swindle Elvis Presley on an airplane deal. He'd tried to screw the King!

With all the corruption charges and scandals swirling around Congress, it's a good thing they've got someone briefing new members on ethics rules. And guess who was supposed to be the teacher? Yup . . . Bob Ney! We kid you not. As the saying goes, those who can, do, and those who can't, teach. Bravely, Innocent Bob thought it best that he temporarily step aside as chairman of the Administration Committee, so someone else will now teach "ethics" to the next eager class of incoming House freshmen.

One can only hope this nasty business is resolved without a trip to Club Fed. Besides the tragic miscarriage of justice, imagine Bob's embarrassment when he discovers, as his fellow Ohioan Jim Traficant learned, that hairpieces are a fashion "don't" in prison. We're sure he's attached to the furry critter that sits atop his head—talk about muskrat love!

Good luck, Sir Dupe.

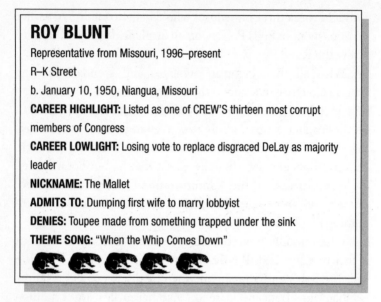

ROY BLUNT

Representative from Missouri, 1996–present

R–K Street

b. January 10, 1950, Niangua, Missouri

CAREER HIGHLIGHT: Listed as one of CREW'S thirteen most corrupt members of Congress

CAREER LOWLIGHT: Losing vote to replace disgraced DeLay as majority leader

NICKNAME: The Mallet

ADMITS TO: Dumping first wife to marry lobbyist

DENIES: Toupee made from something trapped under the sink

THEME SONG: "When the Whip Comes Down"

Missouri's own folksy Roy Blunt may not be as creepy as Tom DeLay, but it's not for lack of trying. Someday a jury of his peers, either in a court, on an ethics committee, or in hell, may come to the conclusion that if DeLay was worse, it was only because he got there first.

You probably think legislation is crafted, considered, and decided upon by the elected representatives of the American people. In fact, that is rarely the case these days in the House, unless it's a resolution to agree that puppies are cute (and even then the lobbyists will carve out a little "earmarked" money for R&D on a new kitty litter). On every major piece of legislation, Roy Blunt unleashes his swarm of lobbyists to make deals for votes. Picture the Kiss Army in Gucci loafers, and know that it was the evil genius of Roy "The Mallet" Blunt that started them marching.

When Tom "The Hammer" DeLay was majority whip, he made Roy his deputy whip, and when DeLay moved up to majority leader, Roy slid into his old slot. Like his idol DeLay, the

Mallet is a major fundraiser, with his own adorably named ROYB (Rely On Your Beliefs) PAC, which doles out hundreds of thousands of dollars to his favorite candidates.

And while Roy has been the King of K Street, mobilizing his brigade of lobbyists to work as deputy whips on important House votes, he's only a small player in the Abramoff world. His ROYB PAC got eighty-five hundred dollars from Abramoff and friends. It may just be luck that he, like so many of his GOP colleagues, wrote a couple of letters to the Bush administration urging them to reject licenses for some Louisiana Indian casinos, which would have been competitors of some of Abramoff's Indian clients. We're sure he was motivated purely by his long-standing opposition to gambling, as his spokesman said.

Roy is up to his eyeballs in connections with DeLay's political piggy bank, ARMPAC, beginning with a *Three's Company* kind of setup in a Washington townhouse. He and DeLay both put their PACs there, and so did the political consulting group they both used, the Alexander Strategy Group. DeLay's wife Christine worked there in the Chrissie role, but we don't know who played Jack or Janet. The Alexander Group was so tainted by Abramoff slime that it's been forced to close down.

Mr. Blunt, like Mr. DeLay, is a reliable defender of Christian family values. Against gay marriage, antichoice, pro-family all the way. So it must have been almost as surprising to his constituents as it was to his wife when old Roy decided to jettison his marriage of more than thirty years for a Philip Morris lobbyist named Abigail Perlman. According to the ethics watchdog group CREW (Citizens for Responsibility and Ethics in Washington), the first thing the Mallet did after assuming the whip post—and before people knew he was dating Abigail—was try to insert legislation in a homeland security bill that would have benefited Philip Morris. Maybe he was planning to bring her flowers, but at the last minute thought it

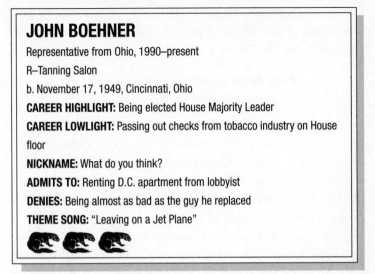

JOHN BOEHNER

Representative from Ohio, 1990–present

R–Tanning Salon

b. November 17, 1949, Cincinnati, Ohio

CAREER HIGHLIGHT: Being elected House Majority Leader

CAREER LOWLIGHT: Passing out checks from tobacco industry on House floor

NICKNAME: What do you think?

ADMITS TO: Renting D.C. apartment from lobbyist

DENIES: Being almost as bad as the guy he replaced

THEME SONG: "Leaving on a Jet Plane"

House GOP Gets a Boehner

Hey, it's pronounced "Bayner," okay? It rhymes with "trainer," not, you know, "donor." At first we thought we should show him some respect just for getting through high school with a name like Boehner (teacher calling attendance the first day of school each year must have been brutal). But then we wondered about his position on Roe (does he pronounce it "row," or "ray"?) and decided the hell with it.

With Tom DeLay sidelined by a pesky ethics indictment and Roy "The Mallet" Blunt seen as Tom's clone, John Boehner must have seemed like a knight in shining armor. He rode in to rescue his party, promising to scrub out the corruption that had left stripes in the House GOP's tighty-whities. But if you look behind the perma-tan, the reformer has a lot in common with the Corruption Crew.

To be fair, he is an improvement in some ways; he doesn't appear to be wearing a "hair system" on top of his head, and he hasn't dumped his wife for a lobbyist mistress. And Lord knows we're grateful he didn't show up for the Capitol Hill coronation of the Reverend Sun Myung Moon, as some of his colleagues did. But Boney is not exactly a breath of fresh air.

Every Ballot Counts in Leadership Vote—
Sometimes More Than Once

We hope it's not a hint of future troubles that he was chosen majority leader in an election distinguished by ballot irregularities—to wit, more ballots cast than people voting. (Gee, who'd'a thought it—a Republican election run by an Ohioan—Debbie Pryce—where there were voting problems. Where's Diebold when you need them?)

The Bone-man got to Congress by defeating a certified sleazeball, Donald "Buz" Lukens, who had been caught having sex with an underage girl. He made his mark right away as one of the Gang of Seven who declared war on the Terror of Bounced Checks, and saved the nation from the tragedy of the House Banking Scandal. For a while, he was one of Newt's boys, pushing the Contract with America. But later, he was part of the failed attempt to overthrow Newt. The next year, Boehner was out as chairman of the Republican conference and relegated to a life as the congressman the cable news shows called when they couldn't book the guy they really wanted.

Working out of the limelight, he did pretty well for himself. Apparently, his motto is "have golf clubs, will travel," as he's gone on some forty-two privately funded trips, according to the Center for Public Integrity. And we're talking *nice* trips—Rome, Scotland, Barcelona, Venice, lots of great destinations, all adding up to more than a hundred fifty thousand dollars' worth of free travel and enough frequent-flyer mileage to be on the president's planned flight to Mars. Maybe that's why when Denny Hastert timidly suggested banning travel on private industry's dime, the Bone-man gave him the stink-eye.

The Bonester got into hot water back in 1995 for passing

out tobacco industry checks to members of the House right on the House floor. He says that it was a mistake and he's sorry, and we're sure that's true. It was technically not illegal, but it looked so . . . payoffy. Can't you just picture one of the old-timers grabbing him by the forearm and leading him into a dark corner? *Whoa, dude, ix-nay on the ash-cay.* (We couldn't help but notice that in the last five years, he *has* accepted dozens of free rides on tobacco-company jets.)

He got a lot slicker when he started hanging around the lobbying world. In fact, during his first turn in the magic power circle, he was the very first Mayor of K Street. He'd meet with lobbyists once a week. Hell, he's renting an apartment from one of them now. Probably nobody in Congress has more of his former staffers working as lobbyists now than Mr. Bones. He practically invented the revolving door to the lobby.

We know we should be grateful—at least Roy Blunt is Boney's bitch, not the other way around. And if we're lucky, he'll spend more of his time in a tanning bed than in bed with lobbyists. We just pray he doesn't stub a toe (pronounced "tay"?) on his way back to the dressing room.

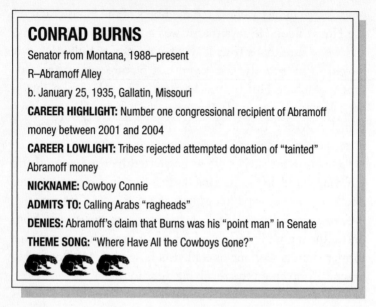

CONRAD BURNS

Senator from Montana, 1988–present

R–Abramoff Alley

b. January 25, 1935, Gallatin, Missouri

CAREER HIGHLIGHT: Number one congressional recipient of Abramoff money between 2001 and 2004

CAREER LOWLIGHT: Tribes rejected attempted donation of "tainted" Abramoff money

NICKNAME: Cowboy Connie

ADMITS TO: Calling Arabs "ragheads"

DENIES: Abramoff's claim that Burns was his "point man" in Senate

THEME SONG: "Where Have All the Cowboys Gone?"

To say I am in favor of spraying pesticides in the faces of pregnant women and infants is not only ludicrous, but offensive.

—CONRAD BURNS, explaining a vote to loosen
EPA restrictions on pesticide testing on humans

In 1988 Cowboy Conrad Burns rode into the Senate as an outsider; now, he's trying to avoid being run off as an outlaw. And we mean outlaw in that macho Wild West way, not, you know, that he's corrupt. Still, there are certain facts that he's had to account for. For one thing, Connie stands head and shoulders above his colleagues when it comes to taking Abramoff money—he was the number one recipient between 2001 and 2004. Not that there's anything wrong with that, necessarily.

But let's face it, ever since he was named to the "13 Most Corrupt Members of Congress" list in 2005 by Citizens for Responsibility and Ethics in Washington, Connie has spent most of his time defending his honor, first by explaining why he didn't need to return the roughly one hundred fifty thousand dollars given to him by Jack Abramoff's clients, then by doing campaign ads that claim Abramoff fooled him and everybody else, too. Frankly, he sounds a little bitter:

> *This Abramoff guy is a bad guy . . . I wish he'd never been born, to be right honest with you.*

Here's what Jack Abramoff says about Conrad Burns, in a *Vanity Fair* interview from April 2006:

> *Every appropriation we wanted [from Burns's committee] we got. Our staffs were as close as they could be. . . . It's a little difficult for him to run from that record.*

And what is that record, exactly? Well, here are the allegations:

The Indian Giver: The accusation is that in exchange for Abramoff-related money, Burns used his power to help a Michigan tribe (and Abramoff client) get three million dollars in government funds. The money was supposed to go to schools for poorer tribes, not to the Saginaw Chippewas, who are, in fact, one of the richest tribes in the nation, thanks to (you guessed it) their casino gambling revenue. But if you're going to imply that Abramoff's money bought influence, well, Conrad is offended. He says the request for the money came from Michigan's two senators, not Abramoff. The problem with that denial appears to be that it isn't true. Letters from the two senators were written a month after Burns started pushing the money toward the Saginaw Chippewas. But hey, you know how dicey the mail can be sometimes.

Sweatshops? No Sweat: Suspicious souls claim that Connie, after getting cash from a representative of the Mariana Islands, another Abramoff client, changed his position on labor regulations there. But Burns must have decided on his own that he wasn't opposed to sweatshop labor after all, because he denies being influenced by Abramoff.

For the record, Mr. Burns says Mr. Abramoff is a liar.

Cronyism: Two of Burns's staffers went to the Super Bowl in 2001 in a corporate jet paid for by Abramoff, and other staffers shuttled back and forth between Abramoff's office and Burns's staff.

This has been a rough time for the Big Guy from the Big Sky, but he's weathered tough storms before. There was that uproar when he told the *Bozeman Daily Chronicle* how challenging it was to live in Washington, what with all the black people. And then there was the time back in 1999 when he called Arabs "ragheads." Even though he apologized, the government of Pakistan canceled a huge order of wheat. How was he supposed to know back then how sensitive Arabs were? And speaking of sensitive, how about that young woman in Billings who was offended when Connie pointed to her nose ring and asked her what tribe she was from?

But nothing beats those crybaby environmentalists. When he voted to allow the testing of pesticides on humans, including pregnant women and kids, he got quite an earful from them. There had been a ban on that kind of testing, but the moratorium ended in 2003, and the Bush administration has allowed the EPA to go back to blasting human guinea pigs with toxic chemicals. It wasn't like Connie wanted to do it:

> I understand, nobody likes the idea of human dos-
> ing . . . if we could get around it, if there was any sure
> way we could get around it, we would. I don't like it
> either. But nonetheless, as we talk about this, we are
> holding up testing on the world around us. We cannot af-
> ford to lose any time or information.

You see? Conrad is a sensitive guy who just has the best in-terest of science in mind. His vote had nothing to do with lob-bying from the pesticide industry, or the thousands of dollars they contributed to his campaigns. No wonder Montanans elected him to represent them. Unless of course it's because of the crystal-meth epidemic in the state.

Classics from the
Republican Reading Room

HARD LINE *by Richard Perle*

Richard Perle, as many of you remember, was an assistant secretary of defense. Known fondly as the "Prince of Darkness," he was the head of the Defense Advisory Board in the early W. years and was one of the proud architects of the Iraq war, which he confidently predicted would be over in a matter of months. His way with words clearly extends to his novel-writing style. Here we meet Defense Department operative "Michael Waterman" and his wife, Laura. This book was published in 1992.

*B*Y EARLY EVENING THEY'D WANDERED BACK TO *the house hand in hand, reconciled by Waterman's pledges to move the family up a notch in the competition for time and attention and by Laura's forbearance in accepting that he meant what he promised. The truth was they loved each other; Michael's government service was a trial they were resolved to endure. . . . He and Laura shared the guest room out behind the house that night. The next day they left together for Aspen.*

Reviewers described Perle's book with phrases like "told in stupefying detail" and "all the breezy charm and subtle thrills of a Nixon memoir." We'd say "Don't quit your day job," but for the sake of humanity, we would dearly love to see him retire to a life of writing. At least bad novels don't kill anybody.

7

THE EMPTY SUITS

Hello? Hello? Anybody In There?

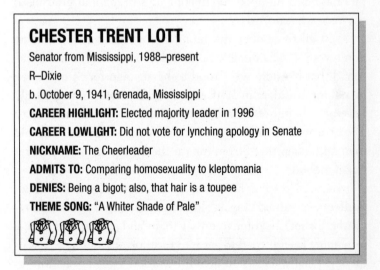

CHESTER TRENT LOTT

Senator from Mississippi, 1988–present

R–Dixie

b. October 9, 1941, Grenada, Mississippi

CAREER HIGHLIGHT: Elected majority leader in 1996

CAREER LOWLIGHT: Did not vote for lynching apology in Senate

NICKNAME: The Cheerleader

ADMITS TO: Comparing homosexuality to kleptomania

DENIES: Being a bigot; also, that hair is a toupee

THEME SONG: "A Whiter Shade of Pale"

It never was easy for me. I was born a poor black child. I remember the days sitting on the porch with my family, singing and dancing, down in Miss'ippi.

—TRENT LOTT

Okay, you caught us, that isn't Trent Lott speaking, it's Steve Martin's character in *The Jerk*. It's probably the only crazy thing Trent didn't say on his "I'm Sorry" Tour as he tried to take back a bad "joke" that revealed his Dixiecrat heart. He didn't succeed in saving his ass or his reputation, but watching him apologize over and over for statements he clearly didn't regret was almost as funny as watching *The Jerk*. Or maybe we *were* watching the jerk.

The fact is, Trent Lott is one of our favorite Republicans. He's such a great example of the clueless Southern good ol' boy. The GOP hates it when their past comes back to haunt them, and Trent Lott is definitely haunting them. Ever since he lost his majority leader position, he's become the stalker of the Republican Party, showing up unexpectedly to apologize and beg for another chance, publicly oversharing his emotional torment at being dumped and making no secret about plotting to get back what he lost.

You all remember the blunder that cost him his power, don't you? Proclaiming at a birthday party for Strom Thurmond that his state was proud to have voted for Strom when he ran for president in 1948 and that the whole country would have been better off if he had won. Trent tried to chalk it up to a joke, a way of ingratiating himself with a hundred-year-old man, but given that Strom ran on the segregationist Dixiecrat ticket, nobody was laughing.

Trent tried to make amends—again, and again, and again. Staffers were afraid to walk alone to their cars, or get into an elevator, for fear he'd lunge out at them and apologize. His few remaining friends tried to get him to stop, told him he was wallowing. Finally, television host Ed Gordon agreed to let him in to make an apology (his fifth!) on a Black Entertainment Television program. That was when Trent's shame spiral hit rock bottom, and he announced his career-deathbed conversion: He now favored affirmative action, and a federal holiday for Dr.

Martin Luther King, Jr.'s birthday. And, thankfully, our long national nightmare was over; Trent stopped apologizing.

Unfortunately, although he stopped saying he was sorry, a whole lot of people didn't start forgiving him. They had their reasons:

- It turned out he'd said almost the exact same thing about Strom twenty years earlier.

- It was also revealed that in college, when he wasn't leading the pep squad at Ole Miss, he'd fought hard to keep his fraternity segregated.

- And then there was his support for Bob Jones University, despite its ban on interracial dating.

- Oh, and he voted against the extension of the Voting Rights Act in 1982.

- And in 1984, speaking at a Sons of Confederate Veterans convention, he said the spirit of Jefferson Davis lived on in the 1984 Republican Party platform.

- Finally, he reportedly gave the keynote address at a 1992 national executive board meeting of the Council of Conservative Citizens, which the Anti-Defamation League describes as the successor to the old white Citizens Councils, and whose agenda is white supremacy.

It just didn't look good, even to Republicans. He had to quit as Senate majority leader.

And even *that* wasn't enough for critics. "What do I need to do, lay down on the floor and flagellate myself?" he was quoted as asking a reporter.

Well, no, but it might have been helpful if you'd shown up, just months later, to vote in favor of the Senate bill that apologized for the nation's lynchings.

And then there's the way you've behaved around the man who took your throne as majority leader, Bill Frist. Maybe if you had just done the modern thing, say, drink 'n' dial and leave a bitter rant on Frist's answering machine instead of writing a tell-all memoir, the whole world wouldn't know that you still didn't get what you'd done wrong. You describe your mistake as "innocent" and say that Frist betrayed you. Whoa—awkward TMI, Trent. And there was this bit about the president, when he called to apologize for "rumors" that the White House had helped push you out and you replied:

> *Thank you, Mr. President, but the rumors did hurt me and you didn't help when you could have.*

Ooh, snap, Mr. President. Senator, we're sure that even now, you're in your den, having a bourbon and plotting your triumphant return to power just as soon as that bitch Frist quits. Maybe you're surrounded by photos of yourself from back in that happier time, when a little nostalgia for Jim Crow was perfectly understandable and not worth getting your bloomers all in a bunch. We know you remain mystified about where it all went so wrong for you, which pretty much guarantees future hilarity. That's why we're rooting for you, our favorite Senator Clueless, to be reelected. We know you won't disappoint us.

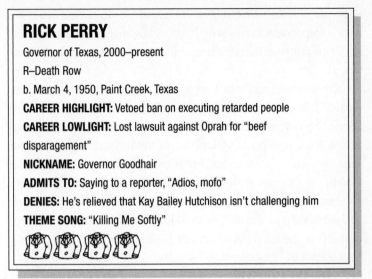

RICK PERRY

Governor of Texas, 2000–present

R–Death Row

b. March 4, 1950, Paint Creek, Texas

CAREER HIGHLIGHT: Vetoed ban on executing retarded people

CAREER LOWLIGHT: Lost lawsuit against Oprah for "beef disparagement"

NICKNAME: Governor Goodhair

ADMITS TO: Saying to a reporter, "Adios, mofo"

DENIES: He's relieved that Kay Bailey Hutchison isn't challenging him

THEME SONG: "Killing Me Softly"

We rarely hand out more than three empty suits to any politician, no matter how dumb. But how to resist a special commendation for a holier-than-thou family values dude who ends a television interview by saying to the reporter, "Adios, mofo"? Texas governor Rick Perry earned his first three empty suits the day reporters caught him practicing his gavel-pounding technique alone in the state senate chamber. (Let's see: up, down, bang! Is that how you do it?) He was about to become lieutenant governor at the time, and wanted to be real slick when he used the gavel in real senate sessions. Practice makes perfect!

The Texecutioner

Speaking of perfect, Texas is proud to lead the nation in executions. And Rick Perry showed early on he would do whatever it takes to maintain that lead, even if it meant killing some retarded people. He vetoed a bill that would have banned execution of the mentally retarded. And in 2004, when Houston law enforcement officials called for a moratorium on executions until they could sort out gross irregularities in their crime lab, Rick's response was to shrug it off. *Adios, mofo,* was his attitude about death row inmates who might have been wrongly convicted.

Of course, you can't execute *everybody* who does you wrong. Like, Oprah Winfrey. When she did a show in 1996 about the potential dangers of mad cow disease in the United States, Rick was Texas agriculture secretary, and when she said she wouldn't eat another burger, well, those were fighting words. Don't mess with Texas cattle, that was Rick's motto. He wanted the state attorney general to sue her under the new "perishable food disparagement" law. The attorney general refused, but the cattle growers sued. They lost, of course, partly because what her expert said was true, and partly because even in Rick Perry's Texas, the First Amendment still applies.

It's setbacks like that one that make a man glad he has God on his side, and Jesus is most definitely Rick's chief of staff. We don't begrudge a guy his faith, even when he says scary things like "intelligent design is a valid scientific theory" that should be taught in science class along with real scientific theory like, say, evolution. But it's a bit off-putting to learn that he prays in the middle of staff meetings, as he told an interviewer in ChristiaNet. (At least it explains the lips moving.) And we aren't sure we're comfortable with the subtle invitation he sent out recently. He was traveling to a Christian school to sign anti-abortion and anti–gay marriage legislation, and Team Texecutioner wanted a good crowd. Here's how they put it:

> We want to completely fill this location with pro-family Christian friends who can celebrate with us.

When some people complained that he was using a tax-exempt religious facility for a political event, a Perry spokesman said, "It's not limited to people of one faith." As long as whatever faith they practice is Christianity.

In fact, Governor Mofo is all about inclusion, except of course for gay people who want equal rights. And that goes for you gay veterans, too. He was asked what he'd tell gay vets returning to Texas from the war, vets who might not be coming home to the same rights as other Texans. His answer:

> *Texans made a decision about marriage and if there's a state that has more lenient views than Texas, then maybe that's a better place for them to live.*

We're hoping that Texans are going to make a decision about Governor Goodhair, too, and we're hoping it ends with "Adios, mofo."

GEORGE ALLEN

Senator from Virginia, 2001–present

R–Copenhagen

b. March 8, 1952, Whittier, California

CAREER HIGHLIGHT: Was compared favorably to Ronald Reagan by Rush Limbaugh

CAREER LOWLIGHT: Flip-flopped on support for hate crimes legislation

NICKNAMES: Chewbacca; Senator Spit Cup

ADMITS TO: Insensitivity for declaring Confederate History Month in Virginia with no references to slavery

DENIES: That the Confederate flag in his home is an emblem of racism

THEME SONG: "Carry Me Back to Old Virginny"

Hey, listen up, Republicans! We've got the answers to your presidential prayers for 2008. White guy (natch), good hair and teeth, slightly Southern, and he's got a name that's already famous. Okay, we admit, he isn't all that bright, but we'll just surround him with grown-ups who know the score. What could possibly go wrong?

Yes, it's beginning to look like a right-wing *Groundhog Day*, where the same waking nightmare is repeated over and over and over again. In this case, it's choosing an empty suit and trying to get him elected because they think he's electable. Just like, all together now: *George W. Bush*. And this time, if the election ends up in the Supreme Court, it's a stone lock.

Feeling queasy yet? You will be when you learn some more about Senator George Allen, a definite frontrunner for 2008.

What could stop his quest for the Republican nomination? It might be his mouth, which is usually full of either chewing tobacco or his foot, or both. (He enjoys Copenhagen smokeless tobacco, in case you want to send him some.)

Chewbacca maintains a worshipful relationship with the man who puts the "mental" in fundamentalist, Pat Robertson. Pat's Kingdom on Earth is Virginia Beach, and that makes him Senator Chewbacca's constituent. Most people would feel awkward slobbering on Robertson's ring, given his ever-more-frequent tendency to make deranged declarations. But not our George. Right after Robertson proclaimed that activist judges were a greater threat to America than "bearded terrorists flying planes into buildings," Chewbacca gave the commencement address at Pat's Regent University. When he was given the opportunity to put a little distance between himself and Pat's rant, he demurred, mumbling something about Pat's comments being taken out of context. (He was right—in context they were even crazier.) For his part, Kooky Pat has judged that George Allen would be an outstanding pawn, er, president.

George Allen grew up in the reflected glare of the spotlight on his father, legendary Washington Redskins coach George Allen. He wasn't brought up to be a redneck, but he adopted some of the trappings as an adult—like the decorative noose hanging from a tree at his law office, and a Confederate flag hanging in his home. The noose was just a symbol of "Western justice," kind of a cute joke, he explained. Nothing to do with racism.

As for the flag, well, as governor, every year he declared April to be Confederate History and Heritage Month. The Civil War, according to the declaration, was a struggle for "independence and sovereign rights." For white people. And did we mention that he labeled the NAACP an extremist group?

Last summer, he tried to compensate for the "insensitivity" of honoring slaveholders by sponsoring a measure in the Senate that formally apologized for lynching.

So what does that make him—a reformed bigot, or a dangerously clueless dolt? Or a guy trying to clean up his messy act before running for president?

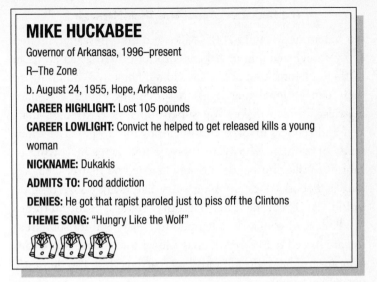

MIKE HUCKABEE

Governor of Arkansas, 1996–present

R–The Zone

b. August 24, 1955, Hope, Arkansas

CAREER HIGHLIGHT: Lost 105 pounds

CAREER LOWLIGHT: Convict he helped to get released kills a young woman

NICKNAME: Dukakis

ADMITS TO: Food addiction

DENIES: He got that rapist paroled just to piss off the Clintons

THEME SONG: "Hungry Like the Wolf"

Hi, I'm Mike Huckabee of Arkansas wanting to say, congratulations, Canada, for preserving your national igloo.

> —actual TV message to Canada,
> after "learning" their parliament building is made of ice

We *do not* heart Huckabee, despite the evidence that it's easy to play a practical joke on him. True, he seems like a nice enough guy, and there are a lot of Republicans who think he'd make an excellent candidate for president. His dramatic weight-loss story of being one of those Southern-fried fatties who gets a health scare and then loses more than a hundred pounds is worthy of Oprah, or at least Ricki Lake. Then, like Oprah (if she were a sanctimonious and homophobic white guy), he goes around the country proselytizing. And in this case, we don't mean just about losing weight.

Mike was a Baptist minister before running for lieutenant governor. He says he's never sipped a beer, and that his body belongs to the Lord. We pray the Lord doesn't mind stretch marks.

The Huckabees Super-Size Their Marriage

On Valentine's Day in 2005, Mike and his wife, Janet, invited every straight couple in Arkansas to join them at an arena in Little Rock for a kind of mass wedding. They were bumping up their conventional marriages to something called "covenant marriage," which makes you super-duper extra-strength married and renders divorce almost impossible to get. The thousands of women who were there joined Janet in vowing to submit to their husbands and stay married no matter what. As long as nobody does anything crazy like drink booze or, God forbid, dance, covenant marriage, they say, is a beautiful thing.

Unless, of course, you happen to be gay and for some reason are forced to live in Arkansas. Governor Huckabee presides over a state that bans not only gay marriage, but also domestic partnership rights.

Huckabee Hears a Horton—Who? (Willie Horton, That's Who)

If Mike does decide to run for president, his religious practices will be the least of his worries. He's considered to be partially responsible for the parole of a convicted rapist who then went on to kill at least one woman, maybe two, in Missouri. The sordid tale of Wayne Dumond is pure Southern Gothic, complete with rape, castration, and charges of corruption. Dumond was accused of raping a distant cousin of then-governor Clinton, whose right-wing nutbag enemies assumed Dumond was being framed by Clinton or his friends. While home awaiting trial on the rape charge, Dumond was assaulted by thugs who castrated him. His testicles, it is reported, were put on display by the local sheriff. (Clearly that guy was not Andy of Mayberry.) As soon as Huckabee became governor, he said, he'd commute Dumond's sentence to time served. But the protests that erupted slowed him down. Months later, on the same day the parole board granted Dumond a parole, Huckabee denied clemency. Oops—too late. Dumond was paroled to Missouri, where even without balls he managed to commit murder. He died of cancer in a Missouri jail.

So, although the governor can *technically* insist it wasn't his fault, you can see how this could be kind of a Willie Horton problem. . . .

Christian Bulimia

Mike has other issues he'll have to overcome if he wants to be president. For one thing, Dumond wasn't the only convict who got a "get out of jail free" pass. Huckabee has commuted the sentences of more than a hundred convicts, including a dozen murderers. The one most likely to doom his presidential hopes: one Glen Martin Green.

In 2004, Huckabee announced plans to grant clemency to Green, who was convicted of killing an eighteen-year-old pregnant woman. Her body was found in a swamp. She had been beaten and run over by a car. Huckabee had heard from Green's minister that he thought Green was innocent. The ensuing outrage forced Governor Dukakabee to back down and had the locals wondering why all the clemencies.

We'd chalk it up to Christian forgiveness, except that in fact it's more like Christian bulimia. You see, while he binged on clemencies, he also purged on executions. Mike's had at least a dozen people executed, including a schizophrenic prisoner who had to be forcibly medicated to make him fit for lethal injection.

Finally, no doubt he was just being friendly to our neighbors to the north, but it will be amusing to see whether Mike can live down the joke played on him by a Canadian television reporter. A tricky Canuck named Rick Mercer convinced Mike that Canada's parliament building was made entirely of ice. Canadian TV viewers were treated to a smiling Mike saying,

"Hi, I'm Mike Huckabee of Arkansas wanting to say, congratulations for preserving your national igloo." We saw the clip with our own eyes—and we're sure Mike should be praying this hilarious sound bite doesn't show up in some rival's campaign commercial.

He's another man from Hope, and he gives us the Willies.

PART THREE
THE WARMONGERS

8

MAKE MONEY, NOT LOVE

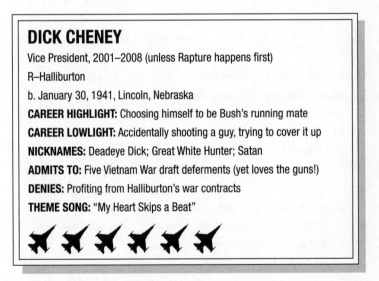

DICK CHENEY

Vice President, 2001–2008 (unless Rapture happens first)

R–Halliburton

b. January 30, 1941, Lincoln, Nebraska

CAREER HIGHLIGHT: Choosing himself to be Bush's running mate

CAREER LOWLIGHT: Accidentally shooting a guy, trying to cover it up

NICKNAMES: Deadeye Dick; Great White Hunter; Satan

ADMITS TO: Five Vietnam War draft deferments (yet loves the guns!)

DENIES: Profiting from Halliburton's war contracts

THEME SONG: "My Heart Skips a Beat"

We have to believe that in the secret corner of Dick's heart, the part that doesn't show up on an angiogram, his very favoritest day of this whole administration was the morning of

June 29, 2002. That was the day he got to be president of the United States, for real. His "term" lasted for almost three golden hours while George W., the boy king, was having a colonoscopy.

Unfortunately for Dick, all they found up Bush's ass was his head—no chance for Darth Cheney to assume the presidency on a long-term basis. But that was fine with him. He pretty much runs the administration anyway, convincing the president that he's right about, well, everything. And yet, he's wrong so much of the time. Let's just take Iraq as an example:

We will be greeted as liberators . . . the people of Iraq will welcome us as liberators. . . . I think it will go relatively quickly . . . [in] weeks rather than months.

—on MEET THE PRESS, March 16, 2003

We believe [Saddam] has in fact reconstituted nuclear weapons.

—on MEET THE PRESS, March 16, 2003

I think there has been fairly significant success in terms of putting Iraq back together again. The price we've had to pay is not out of line and certainly wouldn't lead me to suggest or think that the strategy is flawed or needs to be changed.

—on MEET THE PRESS, September 14, 2003

It goes back to the early nineties. It involves a whole series of contacts, high-level contacts with Osama bin Laden and Iraqi intelligence officials.

—on CNBC, June 17, 2004 (discussing the "overwhelming" evidence of a connection between Bin Laden and Iraq)

I think they're in the last throes, if you will, of the insurgency.

—on LARRY KING LIVE, June 20, 2005

The press, with all due respect, [is] often times lazy, often times simply reports what somebody else in the press said without doing their homework.

—on CNBC, June 17, 2004

The American press is all about lies! All they tell is lies, lies and more lies!

—(Okay, that one is actually BAGHDAD BOB, Saddam's minister of information)

That seems like a lot of mistakes, especially when you consider that it's simply a tasting menu from the rich bounty of Cheney screwups and miscalculations, and we aren't just talking about Iraq. Dick's been on the wrong side of history lots of times, like when he voted against a congressional resolution calling for Nelson Mandela's release from prison. But basically, we're talking about a career built on a tower of bullshit.

Secrets and Lies

Secret: Convened a secret energy task force in 2001, which included executives from big oil companies so that they could help formulate the new administration's gigantic giveaways to their industry. Cheney refused to reveal who came to the meetings, fighting all the way to the Supreme Court. (Went duck hunting with Justice Scalia while case was before him. Scalia was not shot.)

Lie: Insisted he'd severed all ties to Halliburton when he ran for vice president. Neglected to mention the 433,000 shares of stock options he continued to own, and the hundreds of thousands of dollars in deferred salary he still collected.

Secret: Indicted former aide Scooter Libby says Cheney told him to leak intelligence information to reporters—while

Cheney and the president pretended to be outraged and eager to find out who was leaking White House secrets.

Lie: Cheney said that when he was chairman of Halliburton he refused to do business with Iraq, even if it was technically legal. In fact, two of Halliburton's subsidiaries did sell more than seventy million dollars' worth of oil production equipment and spare parts to Iraq.

Secret and Lie: As the Vice President for Torture, Dead-eye Dick campaigned hard for the CIA's right to rough up detainees. "The United States does not torture," he said, although some dead detainees might beg to differ, if they could. Congress passed the bill anyway; the president signed it but in a signing statement said it doesn't really apply to him.

Hey, Dick, bet you can't wait for this administration to be over, when it comes right down to it. Just think, no more wimping out to undisclosed locations; no more fear of "the Jackal" getting you, as you told *Vanity Fair,* no more pretending everything is going well when not one single program or strategy or scheme has turned out the way you planned it because of these twits who can run a campaign but couldn't govern a Boy Scout circle jerk. Jesus, no wonder you get so cranky you drop the F-bomb on the Senate floor. Leahy had it coming, the pinko bastard, but the values crowd was not amused. Maybe you should have invited Leahy to go quail hunting.

More Secrets, More Lies, and Some Buckshot

We know you didn't mean to shoot that old guy down in Texas, but we love how your staff tried to keep it a secret. It was so Cheneyish. And then when the cover-up failed, you let other people blame Mr. Whittington. You left the old geezer hanging out there for days before finally accepting responsibility. It was real manly, the way you sought out the white-hot grilling of

Fox News to do it, too, but we never quite understood why you chose to go back to the ranch and eat dinner that fateful day rather than go to the hospital to visit the man you shot. We know some people think you were drunk when you shot him and didn't want to be seen, but we're sure they're just political enemies talking trash. It'll be a relief to get out of the public eye, won't it? Oh, wait, you're never *in* the public eye, unless you want to come out of your lair to set the public crooked about an urgent matter.

Thank goodness you had the foresight to go shopping for a huge estate in Maryland as thousands of your fellow Americans were having their homes destroyed by Katrina and hundreds were dying while they waited for help from your government.

We're gonna miss you, Dick.

DUNCAN HUNTER

Representative from California, 1981–present

R–Pentagon

b. May 31, 1948, Riverside, California

CAREER HIGHLIGHT: Proposed bill to erect fence across U.S.-Mexican border

CAREER LOWLIGHT: Called 9/11 Commission a "traveling circus"

NICKNAMES: Yo-Yo; Slam Duncan

ADMITS TO: Taking huge contributions from defense contractors

DENIES: Selling influence to defense contractors

THEME SONG: "Don't Fence Me In"

Q: Congressman Hunter, what's your response to the prisoner abuse complaints at Guantánamo?

A: Honey glazed chicken.

Q: No, Congressman, perhaps you didn't understand the question. What is your reaction to the acknowledged abuse of some prisoners at the Guantánamo Bay prison?

A: Lemon baked fish.

Q: Congressman Hunter, really, sir, don't you have anything more substantive to say about this situation?

A: Whole wheat pita. Assorted vegetables and fruit.

Yes, those were the answers at a news conference in June 2005, when Congressman Duncan Hunter took questions from reporters about the abuse of prisoners at Guantánamo Bay. Over and over again their questions were answered with what he said were Gitmo menu items provided to him by the U.S. government. It may have been the dramatic climax of a long season of artful cover-ups and justifications for American prisoner abuse, from Guantánamo to Abu Ghraib. The military contractors who contribute so lavishly to him must have been on their feet shouting "Bravo!"

"This century is going to be a very dangerous century," Duncan Hunter declared in 2003 when he reported for duty as the new House Armed Services Committee chairman. And a profitable one, if you're a defense contractor, as so many of Duncan's contributors are, people like the good folks of Boeing and a company called Titan. Now, Titan happens to specialize in sending translators to work in places like Abu Ghraib. Hmm . . . could that be why the Dunkster did everything he could to stifle the investigation into the abuses there?

But Slam Duncan is way more than just a run-of-the-mill congressman who takes money from military contractors who then by pure coincidence get huge government contracts. He is a creative thinker.

Take his cure for the common Mexican. His solution to the illegal immigration problem is to build a fifteen-foot-high fence between the United States and Mexico. A long double fence from the Pacific Ocean to the Gulf of Mexico. For now, he's settled for a seven-hundred-mile double fence at a cost of a couple of billion dollars. The Mexicans call the idea "shameful." Duncan calls it "a start."

In December 2005, while working hard to block the McCain antitorture bill in the House, Duncan must have needed to kick back, relax, and shoot something. And what better place than Santa Rosa Island, one of the beautiful Channel Islands off the California coast? It's part of a national park where hunters can pay to shoot deer (which have been brought to the island just so they can be shot, in fact). Only one part of the island is earmarked for private hunting—the rest is used for less lethal forms of recreation. But Hunter is a hunter, and he wanted it all. He introduced legislation to give the whole island to the military, to make it a private shooting gallery for veterans and servicemen and servicewomen on leave. Of course, they can go to the island now, and the Pentagon says they don't want it. So what was his thinking? Here's what he said:

> *I want to see two things. One is to allow our paralyzed veterans to hunt and fish at Santa Rosa Island as a special place for them, and number two is to stop the extermination plan of deer and elk.*

Let's see if we've got this right. We kill these animals to save them from extermination, is that the idea, Duncan? And do we think a lot of paralyzed veterans have "Get own private hunting island" high on their to-do lists?

Sshhh . . . be vewy, vewy quiet. We're pretty sure there was a campaign contribution in there somewhere.

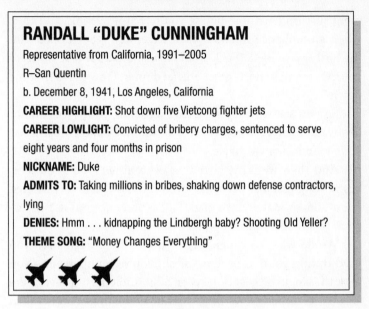

RANDALL "DUKE" CUNNINGHAM

Representative from California, 1991–2005

R–San Quentin

b. December 8, 1941, Los Angeles, California

CAREER HIGHLIGHT: Shot down five Vietcong fighter jets

CAREER LOWLIGHT: Convicted of bribery charges, sentenced to serve eight years and four months in prison

NICKNAME: Duke

ADMITS TO: Taking millions in bribes, shaking down defense contractors, lying

DENIES: Hmm . . . kidnapping the Lindbergh baby? Shooting Old Yeller?

THEME SONG: "Money Changes Everything"

From Top Gun to Prison Bottom!

Hey, Duke, what's the deal? There's no crying in bribery! You're supposed to be Mr. Tough Guy, remember, the Top Gun pilot? Or were you crying because you knew you'd be lucky if you didn't go from Top Gun to top (actually bottom) when you got to the Big House? Watching you blubber as you confessed to being a whore and a thief, we almost, just for a second, felt a little sorry for you. But then we remembered what a bullying asshole you were when you were living high on defense contractors' hogs.

Remember when you said the liberal leadership in Congress should be lined up and shot? Or when you called Bill Clinton a traitor, Tokyo Rose, for taking a student trip to Moscow? Then there was the time you called Congresswoman Pat Schroeder a socialist, and referred to "homos" in the military. And speaking of "homos," how about the time you told a group of prostate cancer survivors that "prostate cancer treatment just isn't natural, unless you're Barney Frank" and then when an audience member took exception, you flipped him the bird and snarled, "Fuck you." How about your first words to your Vietnamese hosts at an official dinner: "You gooks shot me down."

So you see why, for us, Duke, watching you cry is kind of like watching Nixon cry. We feel all squinchy and embarrassed at first, and then we giggle.

And then we remember that even in jail, you get a nice, cushy congressional pension—even though you're a convicted felon—and it makes us so mad that, as you once put it, "we just want to strangle Mary Poppins."

We do want to congratulate you for the imagination you used during your scam. First of all, you're number one—you took the single biggest bribe ever, $2.4 million. And then there was the technique, the "Bribe Menu" as the prosecutors called it. They say the menu shows prospective "customers" the various government contracts that could be ordered, and at what price. Like, that "16" in the first column represents a sixteen-million-dollar contract offered in exchange for a hundred-forty-thousand-dollar boat (see "BT" with the number 140 in the next column). A seventeen-million-dollar contract would cost an additional fifty thou. (Love that it's on House stationery, by the way.)

In June 2003, you got a friendly defense contractor, Mitchell Wade of MZM, to buy your house at a wildly inflated price. And that was only the beginning. There was the yacht called the *Duke Stir*, the antiques, the Persian rugs, and a lot of cash. We've always been partial to the Louis Philippe antique commode, even though we know in this case it's not a toilet. Did your wife pick out all this stuff? Did she ever wonder how you could afford it? Did she think she was especially good at managing the old family budget, or what? Why are we picturing a woman who looks a lot like Carmela Soprano at this point? We've got to hand it to you, Duke. You were a trailblazer. They will retire your number in the Congressional Bribery Arena (has MZM bought the naming rights for that yet?).

We know what the contractors got from Duke in the way of government contracts. But what we don't know, as we write this, is whether they got something worth more than the money—national security secrets. Duke was on the Intelligence Committee, and although it's shocking when you think about it, he was given high security clearance and access to tons of intelligence. What if the guys he was shaking down were actually shaking *him* down—for secrets involving counterterrorism, for example? Maybe the Duke was the Dupe. And investigators have made it clear the Duke is only the first, not the last, big fish they're going to reel in.

Duke, you retire to Club Fed as a champion, the Lou Gehrig of bribe takers. Have a great time, and don't spend your pension on cigarettes at the canteen.

9

THE CHICKEN HAWKS

Representative Tom DeLay

FAILED TO SERVE IN:
Vietnam

REASON:
Too many minorities, no room for him

Nothing is more important in the face of a war than cutting taxes.

—TOM DELAY

So that's where all those Vietnam veterans went wrong. They should have been cutting taxes, not getting shot at in the jungle. If only they'd listened to Tom DeLay. Tom, you see, chose to fight the enemy over here, so that he wouldn't have to fight them over there. Of course, in his case, the enemies were household bugs and garden pests.

Tom sat out part of the war with student deferments, first as a student at Baylor University, which he was asked to leave for reasons he doesn't explain but probably involved the consumption of alcohol, and then as a biology student at the University of Houston. He graduated in 1970 and is believed to have lucked into a very high draft lottery number, allowing him to duck military service. Of course, that's not the reason he reportedly gave for failing to serve.

It turns out there was just no room for a patriotic guy like Tom DeLay in the military, because, he said, poor minority kids had taken all the slots to escape poverty. Besides, he had to get started on his promising career. Just out of college Tom took a job at a pesticide company, where his chores included mixing batches of rat poison. He had a real talent for it.

And just because he didn't go to war doesn't mean he doesn't like to play with guns. Especially if he can surround himself with a "band of brothers" who make generous campaign donations, like the NRA. "When a man is in trouble or in a good fight, you want to have your friends around, preferably armed," he told an NRA banquet.

Yup, when it comes to defending *himself*, Tom does a great job. Defending his country, though, is quite another matter.

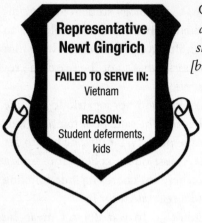

Representative Newt Gingrich

FAILED TO SERVE IN:
Vietnam

REASON:
Student deferments, kids

Given everything I believe in, a large part of me thinks I should have gone over.... [but] Part of the question I had to ask myself was what difference I would have made.

—NEWT GINGRICH, on why he didn't go to Vietnam, in *The Wall Street Journal,* 1985

As you can tell, Newt was tortured by Vietnam. Not enough to *go,* of course, but enough to, you know, wonder if he would have made a difference if he had gone. We can picture him imagining what it would be like to actually experience a war rather than bloviate about one, and then coming to the inescapable conclusion that he was only cut out to fantasize about it.

In Vietnam, we decided that defeat was preferable to the risk of victory, not that we could not win, but the nation, the body politic, after a decade of agonizing internal struggle, decided that defeat was preferable to the cost of victory.

—NEWT GINGRICH, "Principles for Victory," September 2001

Hey, Newt, you know what else was preferable? Making sure your student deferments were in order so you didn't have to go to war. Becoming a father also got you a "hardship" deferment that kept you out of war. Now, chicken hawks are by definition hypocrites, since they're warmongers who wouldn't fight, but you had the giblets to act like a liberal when it came to being drafted, and then later to sneer at liberals and describe them as "counterculture McGoverniks." By the way, McGovern was a decorated war veteran. He was a fighter pilot in WWII. Maybe a more appropriate term for guys like you, who say they believed in the war but still ducked it, would be pro-war chicken-newts.

Actually, Newt Gingrich cared a lot about the war—the Civil War. In fact, he's made a second career out of rewriting it. If only he could have gone to Vietnam in Confederate or Union soldier drag—maybe stage one of those exciting reenactment battles. Of course, make-believe war isn't nearly as scary as the real thing.

Straight from the Warmonger's Mouth: *"If an entire society engaged in the indulgences of an elite few, you could tear the society to shreds."*

Speaking from experience, eh, Newt?

**House Speaker
Denny Hastert**

FAILED TO SERVE IN:
Vietnam

REASON:
Wrestling injuries

It's a lot easier to go mano a mano against sweaty guys in a gymnasium than in the steamy jungles of Vietnam, although we'd assume Hastert would have the heavyweight division almost exclusively to himself. Denny Hastert was at Wheaton College until his graduation in 1964. He had been a star wrestler and played some football, too. Alas, a bum shoulder from injuries sustained while fighting the good fight on a wrestling mat rendered him unfit to serve in Vietnam.

Band of Bothers?

Is he bitter to this day? We can't help but notice how the men who did go to Vietnam seem to rub Denny the wrong way. Take John Kerry's service—apparently, earning Purple Hearts and Bronze and Silver Stars didn't prove Kerry was a tough soldier. Not to Denny Hastert, who said before the 2004 election that al-Qaeda would prefer Kerry as president, because he "would file a lawsuit with the World Court or something, rather than respond with troops." Maybe if Kerry had won an All-State wrestling trophy Hastert would have been satisfied.

Same goes for you, John McCain. All that whining about being a POW, letting other prisoners out before you were released even though you could have been freed sooner, what do you know about sacrificing for your country? When McCain had the nerve to ask why the American people weren't being asked to make sacrifices for the never-ending War on Terror, Denny got all up in his grille and pinned his ass to the mat. Declared Speaker Denny:

*If you want to see sacrifice, John McCain ought to visit
our young men and women at Walter Reed [Army Medical Center] and Bethesda [Naval Hospital]. There's the
sacrifice in this country.*

Did he deliberately miss McCain's point, or is he just stupid? Oh, never mind.

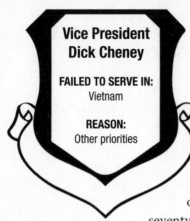

Vice President Dick Cheney

FAILED TO SERVE IN:
Vietnam

REASON:
Other priorities

Dead-eye Dick Cheney is a brave man with a gun, as long as nobody's shooting back. He's only comfortable when the enemy combatant is a defenseless bird and he's just hauled his saggy ass out of an armored car to be a manly man and "hunt" by the side of the road. And if you're a seventy-eight-year-old man who gets in the line of fire, look out, pal. You're going to find out the true meaning of "friendly fire," right in the face.

No way Dick was going to waste his time on a war he couldn't profit from! Beginning with his first deferment in March 1963, he went on to score a *Naked Republicans* record of *five* deferments, the last one granted in 1966 when he was twenty-five years old. After flunking out of Yale (or preferring the rigors of Casper Community College), Dick was briefly 1-A, but it was 1962, and the Army wasn't taking guys his age. Once the war got serious, so did Dick, applying for student deferments *four times* as he matriculated at the University of Wyoming. Finally, out of graduate school and clearly desperate, Dick took advantage of the fact that the Army didn't draft married men with kids. After he impregnated his lovely wife, Lynne, he was able to get a "hardship" deferment, just in time to ensure he'd experience nothing scarier in the sixties than a highway patrolman armed with a Breathalyzer.

Straight from the Warmonger's Mouth: *"I complied fully with all the requirements of the statutes, registered with the draft when I turned eighteen. Had I been drafted, I would have obviously been happy to serve."*

Obviously.

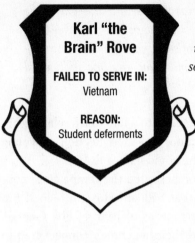

Karl "the Brain" Rove

FAILED TO SERVE IN:
Vietnam

REASON:
Student deferments

There were a lot of legitimate reasons for not going. There were a lot of legitimate reasons for going. . . . But I never heard Karl advocate violating that law. That he didn't go makes him like hundreds of thousands of other guys my age who didn't go.

—Rove high school classmate
MARK GUSTAVSON,
to *The Salt Lake Tribune*

It's just as well Private Turd Blossom didn't go to 'Nam. We can only imagine a serious case of jungle fungus in those doughy fat-boy thighs, which probably would have sent him home anyway. He wasn't the first College Republican to duck the draft with questionable student deferments, and we would chalk it up to typical youthful hypocrisy, which in his case was followed by mature adult hypocrisy, except that he's helped get so damned many people killed.

Rove entered the University of Utah in 1969 and got a student deferment in 1970, which was lucky since he had a low lottery number. But somehow, even when he was only a part-time student and should have been eligible, he didn't get drafted.

His contribution to the war effort was to work, alongside soon-to-be-convicted felon Donald Segretti, for the reelection of über-weasel Richard Nixon. A year later, Rove first laid eyes on Boy George W. Bush, and described the magic moment to *The New Yorker:*

I can literally remember what he was wearing: an Air National Guard flight jacket, cowboy boots, blue jeans,

complete with the—in Texas you see it a lot—one of the
back pockets will have a circle worn in the pocket from
where you carry your tin of snuff, your tin of tobacco. He
was exuding more charisma than any one individual
should be allowed to have.

The man-crush that ensued led to a long-term relationship
with tragic results: the selection, and then election, of young
George. God, how we wish he could have quit him.

In the service of W., he orchestrated the campaign to convince the American people that Saddam Hussein helped Bin
Laden attack on 9/11. After months of hearing Boy George,
Dead-eye Dick, Rummy, and their henchmen connect Iraq to
9/11, two-thirds of the public believed Saddam did everything
except fly one of those jets himself.

Selling of the Iraq war to America: Mission accomplished,
Turd Blossom.

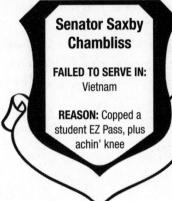

Senator Saxby Chambliss

FAILED TO SERVE IN: Vietnam

REASON: Copped a student EZ Pass, plus achin' knee

If it takes a pair of balls as big as Georgia peaches to be a good soldier, it's really a damned shame Saxby Chambliss ditched the draft. Judging by the cojones he showed during his vicious campaign against then Senator Max Cleland, he would have been a regular Rambo in the jungle.

Saxby graduated from the University of Georgia in 1966 and law school in '68. Throughout college he filed for one student deferment after another, and then he was able to worm his way to a 4-F with a "bum knee." He went to Congress in 1994 and chaired the House Intelligence Subcommittee on Terrorism, but he showed no intelligence about terrorism when he said in November 2001 that the best way to deal with terrorists in Georgia would be to turn a sheriff loose to arrest every Muslim who came into the state.

You would think the voters of Georgia would have rejected him based on that stupidity alone, but then you'd be forgetting that these are the same people who elected Zell Miller.

In 2002 Saxby Chambliss decided to challenge Democratic senator Max Cleland, a veteran who lost three limbs in Vietnam. Chambliss's shameless campaign ads, which featured the faces of Saddam, Bin Laden, and Cleland, questioned Cleland's toughness, for voting against a homeland security bill. He said that Cleland had "broken his oath to protect and defend the Constitution."

Hard to believe, we know, and during the campaign most people thought he was crazy even to try that kind of tactic. But it worked. For this, Saxby Chambliss earns the extra honor of being the *capo di tutti* chicken hawks (or should it be capon *di tutti* capons?).

Straight from the Warmonger's Mouth: *"Those folks who continue to go out front and talk in a negative way about this* [domestic wiretapping] *program may be aiding and abetting the terrorists."*

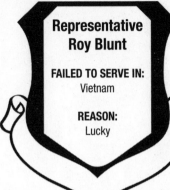

Representative Roy Blunt

FAILED TO SERVE IN:
Vietnam

REASON:
Lucky

When they return, all Americans will owe our soldiers a debt of gratitude for their service in ending the cowardly dictatorship of a madman.

—ROY BLUNT,
on the Iraq war

When it came time to serve his country, Roy Blunt must have asked himself What Would Jesus Do, and realized right away He wouldn't have fought in a pointless war against a made-up enemy, no matter how good the homegrown weed was. That must be why he spent his prime Vietnam years at Southwest Baptist College in Springfield, Missouri.

It was 1967 when he got there, but it might as well have been 1957. There was no free love, no acid, no hippies, and, we're going to assume from looking at what appears to be a "hair appliance" now, no long hair. But there were student deferments. And Roy got himself one. But that wasn't all—in 1969, when the Selective Service held their lottery, Roy lucked out with a high number, and presto!

As for whether to send today's soldiers into harm's way, well, you know how he stands on that. Roy voted to send American troops to Iraq, even predicting that the coalition forces would include more nations than participated in the first Gulf War. Oops. Didn't they teach math back at old Southwest Baptist?

Straight from the Warmonger's Mouth: *"Our freedoms come at a price, and tonight the world is witness to the beginning of the end of tyranny in Iraq and the dawning of a new day for the people of the Gulf region."*

Right. So onward, Christian soldiers.

PART FOUR

THE HALL OF SHAME

They Gave Their All. And They Took Ours.

10

THE LINEUP

Do You Recognize Any of These Men?

If you are appalled, outraged, and disgusted by what you've read so far, take a deep breath; the Hall of Shame is not for the faint of heart. Small children, pregnant women, and people with heart conditions should proceed with the utmost caution. Here you will find some of the most notorious, most dishonest, and most hypocritical Naked Republicans of all time, starting with our newest arrival, Mr. Tom "I Am the Federal Government" DeLay. (Uh, better make that I *was* the federal government, little fella.)

The Hall is modeled after the Baseball Hall of Fame. Baseball, a game where stealing is rewarded, where the owners seek cheap labor from Latin America, and where each game begins with a gaudy vocal display of faux patriotism, has a lot in common with Republicanism. Especially the number one Republican.

It has been said of George W. Bush that he's a guy who was born on third base but thinks he hit a triple. Maybe that's why he loves baseball so much. He was the first president who'd played Little League baseball, and he told Oprah Winfrey that playing Little League in Midland, Texas, was his fondest childhood memory. And back in the pre-9/11 days, when he was adrift, searching for a historical purpose for his administration beyond its certain entry as the first stolen election sanctified by the Supreme Court, he had his Best Idea Ever. Before the Decider became a War President, he decided to be a Tee Ball President, hosting games on the South Lawn of the White House.

Tee ball was the perfect game for him, really. It's designed to make you look coordinated and competent. A nice grown-up gets you all set up to succeed and then hands you the bat. Oh, and you can take an extra swing—you get four, sometimes five, strikes in tee ball. Those are the rules! It's as if Karen Hughes made them up herself with W. in mind.

So come with us now as we pay a visit to the men and women whose lifetime achievements have earned them a hallowed place of dishonor in the Republican Hall of Shame. But first, let's stop and read one of the poems that grace the Hall, inspired by our own president's exploits. (With thanks to "Casey at the Bat.")

DUBYA AT THE BAT

The future wasn't brilliant for the Republicans that day,
The score stood four to two, with but one inning more to play.
Then Cheney was called out at first, and Hastert's fate the same.
Silence fell on the GOP, who suddenly felt lame.

They'd watched their Georgie screw up, from 9/11 to Iraq,
And after Katrina's onslaught, there was no turning back.
He'd made a mess of all he touched with his pampered rich-boy hands.
A rustle of impatience rippled through the nervous stands.

"We'll lose the House! The Senate!" the murmuring began.
"We're screwed for sure if we are forced to run beside this man.

His port deal was ridiculous, the Medicare plan absurd—
Don't give him one more turn at bat, we beg you, Blossom Turd."

On the bench Rove sweated hard, and checked his lineup order
Hoping a Latino star had sneaked across the border.
But none showed up, and he went to bat with only what he had,
And with Santorum, Frist, and Allen, the future did look bad.

But Rick let drive a single, to the wonderment of all,
And old Doc Frist, the softie, tore the cover off the ball;
And when the dust had lifted and they saw what had occurred,
Santorum was on second, and Frist a-huggin' third.

George Allen strode up to the plate, a bat was in his hands,
He spit some chaw and cleaned his cleats as cheers came from the stands.
"He looks so presidential," the crowd began to shout,
"We're in deep trouble, sure enough, but George will pull us out."

Suddenly there came a gasp, as Dubya appeared:
"I make the rules, I'm president, why you lookin' at me so weird?
I'm a wartime prez and I call the shots, I've done it since day one.
Don't worry boys, I'll hit one out, and then we'll have some fun!"

"Aren't you done already?" McCain was heard to sneer,
But Rove was forced to hold him back, 'cause the picture was now clear.
Dubya would bat for sure, and out of turn; no matter,
They'd always brought him everything upon a silver platter.

There was ease in Dubya's manner as he stepped into his place,
There was pride in Dubya's bearing and a smirk upon his face,
And when he spotted Dobson and lightly doffed his hat,
No stranger in the crowd could doubt that Dubya was at bat.

The first pitch sailed in high and tight and barely missed his head.
"This is hard work," said Dubya. "Strike one!" the umpire said.

"Kill the ump, he's a Democrat!" shouted someone in the stand;
And it's likely they'd have killed him had not Dubya raised his hand.

With a smile of Christian charity great Dubya's visage shone;
He stilled the rising tumult; he silenced every moan.
He signaled to the pitcher, and once more the baseball flew;
But Dubya still ignored it, and the umpire called "Strike two!"

"Liberals!" cried the maddened crowds, and someone shouted "Kill!"
But one scornful look from Dubya and the audience was still.
They saw his face grow dazed and scared, like it did in the debate,
And they knew that they were done for, the cruelest twist of fate.

The sneer was gone from Dubya's lip, and how his teeth did grind!
He'd take another mighty swing, with winning still in mind.
And now the pitcher holds the ball, and now he lets it go,
And now the air is shattered by the force of Dubya's blow.

Oh, somewhere in this favored land the sun is shining bright,
Happy days are here again, and somewhere hearts are light;
And somewhere Democrats can laugh, and liberal children shout,
But there is no joy in Crawford—Mighty Dubya has struck out.

Hall of Shame

TOM DELAY
CONGRESSMEN

OPPS

TOM DeLAY

Representative from Texas, 1984–disgraced retirement 2006

Played by his own rules, and then broke some of them

b. April 8, 1947, Laredo, Texas

CAREER HIGHLIGHT: House majority leader

CAREER LOWLIGHT: Forced to resign from House leadership, forced to resign from Congress, forced to defend himself in money-laundering indictment

NICKNAMES: The Hammer; The Natural

PERSONAL BEST: Smiling for mug shot despite humiliation

PERSONAL WORST: Denied being close friend of Jack Abramoff

THEME SONG: "Sympathy for the Devil"

> A slugger who lost his power, and then his love for the game

*Because I care so deeply about this district and the people in it, I
refuse to allow liberal Democrats an opportunity to steal this seat
with a negative, personal campaign.*

　　　　　—TOM DELAY'S farewell message to his constituents

That kind of says it all, doesn't it? What the rest of America calls "winning," the Hammer calls "stealing." Surprising, too, considering that if there was one thing Tom DeLay understood, it was how to manipulate elections.

He really had no choice but to quit. He had become so politically radioactive he was making the hair fall out of his colleagues' toupees. But luckily, by quitting when he did, he can convert his campaign money into his defense fund, and he needs the best lawyers money can buy.

Martyr in the War on Christians

In the words of Baptist minister/crusader Rick Scarborough at his War on Christians conference in March 2006, all of the Natural's problems stem from the fact that he *"takes his faith seriously into public office, which made him a target for all those who despise the cause of Christ."*

Not that the Natural didn't see it all coming. Here's his warning in a conference call to the Family Research Council during the heat of the fight to stop doctors from removing Terri Schiavo's feeding tube:

> *This is exactly the issue that's going on in America, of attacks against the conservative movement, against me and many others. The point is, the other side has figured out how to win and defeat the conservative movement, and that is to go after people personally, charge them with frivolous charges, link that up with all these do-gooder organizations funded by George Soros, and then get the national media on their side.*

Note, if you will, that liberals have figured out how to defeat the conservative movement (obviously using the element of surprise, since to the casual observer, conservatives control all three branches of government). And then note how it becomes all about Tom, accused of "frivolous charges" supported by George Soros and the national media. Masterful work, really.

On Family Values

The Natural was Mr. Family Values, and to the extent that he paid his wife and daughter half a million dollars over the past four years to work for him, he was quite a provider. Of course, when anybody questions whether he is unethically shoveling money at family members, the Natural mutates instantly into a victim again:

> *My wife and daughter have any right, just like any other American, to be employed and be compensated for their employment. . . . It's pretty disgusting, particularly when my wife and daughter are singled out and others are not, in similar situations in the Senate and as well as the House.*

Way to stand up for your family, Tom. But how about the rest of your family, like your mother, and your brothers and sister? Remember them? Not so much? Here's a hint: They're the ones you don't speak to anymore, or allow to contact you, or invite to family functions like your daughter's wedding. Ring a bell?

Why He Was Called the Hammer: It Wasn't for His Cabinetmaking Skills

The Hammer was a well-known bully whose threats sometimes (almost) got him in trouble, if you consider a slap on the wrist from the zombies in the House Ethics Committee to be trouble. His three "admonishments" didn't slow him down for a minute. Here are some of his Greatest Hits from the bully pulpit:

- The K Street coup: *"If you want to play in our revolution, you have to live by our rules,"* Tom said. (The "or else" was silent.) He was talking about lobbyists who might have dared to hire Democrats when positions in their firms opened up. In 1999, he was admonished by the Ethics Committee for threatening a trade group that wanted to hire a Democrat as its president. Result: Most lobbying groups hired only Republicans. It was the K Street way.

- Payback: Republican colleagues who crossed him (that is, voted their own way) feared he would "primary" them—dipping into his huge campaign fund to support a rival Republican candidate in a primary.

- He strong-armed the FAA into helping him track a plane carrying Texas Democrats who had left the state rather than be forced to vote for his redistricting plan for the state. He got an "admonishment" from the Ethics Committee for using government resources for political purposes.

- His third admonishment came when he suggested to Congressman Nick Smith, who was retiring, that he'd endorse Smith's son for the seat if Smith voted DeLay's way on a prescription drug bill.

- The Big Purge: He tried to get the Ethics Committee to weaken its rules, and purged the recalcitrant Republicans who wouldn't go along with his plan.

- Militant smoker: Reportedly, a waitress once asked him to observe the no-smoking rules in a steakhouse. Federal government rules, she said. "I *am* the federal government," the Natural barked back. How sad to have your personal freedom crushed.

- Threatened judges: Speaking of crushing, who can forget the Natural's threats to "activist judges":

The time will come for the men responsible for this to answer for their behavior, but not today.

That time he was talking about the Terri Schiavo case, which allowed him a triple play: bullying, religious extremism, and hypocrisy, since the DeLay family chose to disconnect Tom's father from life support after an accident.

The Natural as Empty Suit

DeLay wasn't terribly smart on matters not pertaining to money or power. Consider his visit to Reliant Park in Houston to visit some of the evacuees from Hurricane Katrina. "Now, tell me the truth, boys, is this kind of fun?" The puzzled kids nodded their heads, and given what they'd been through, probably were secretly praying for the scary man to go away. Actually, he proved his worthiness as an empty suit long ago, when he told the *Houston Chronicle* that it's never been proven that "air toxics are hazardous to people." You'd think a guy who started his career as a bug exterminator would have some understanding of toxins.

DeLies

As for lying, this was the first talent the Natural exhibited when he began playing the game, and the list is long. But we thought it would be fun to read from his letter to constituents, denying that Jack Abramoff was a friend of his:

The notion that Abramoff was a close friend who wielded influence over me is absolutely untrue. Jack Abramoff and I were not close personal friends.

Back on New Year's Eve 1997 in the Mariana Islands, the Natural sang quite a different tune:

> *When one of my closest and dearest friends, Jack Abramoff, your most able representative in Washington, D.C., invited me to the islands, I wanted to see firsthand the free-market success and the progress and reform you have made.*

We'll give you a moment to compose yourselves after that moving tribute. Maybe it will help if you remember that the Hammer is accused of blocking an investigation into sweatshop conditions in the Marianas. All better? Good. Because Mr. Abramoff says in his *Vanity Fair* interview that he and Tom were close, they would sit and chat about religion and opera and golf. In fact, DeLay went to Scotland in 2000 to play golf, all expenses paid . . . by Jack Abramoff. First class all the way, of course, to the tune of fourteen thousand dollars, according to records obtained by ABC News. That would have been a violation of ethics rules, just for the record.

If you want to wallow even more deeply into the muck, ThinkProgress.org is one place to start.

We can't leave the Natural without remembering what the liberal media, the left-wingers, and the radical feminists are accusing him of, in broad terms.

The Indictment

He was indicted in Texas for a money-laundering scheme involving campaign funds for his Texans for a Republican Majority PAC. And in the end, attracting money has been what the Natural excelled at most effortlessly of all.

He raised more than thirty-five million dollars over the last ten years, according to an Associated Press report, and he doled it out to the candidates he wanted to support. That's what made him a kingmaker. Oh, and it also made him a hell of a good-time Tommy, because he dipped freely into those campaign funds himself, jetting to resorts around the world, taking golf trips, eating expensive meals, staying in luxury hotels, you name it. And it may all have been legal—because the laws allow him to use campaign contributions to raise more campaign contributions.

We really are going to miss the Natural. We console ourselves by remembering the cheerful words of War on Christians organizer Rick Scarborough, who said this to Mr. DeLay:

God always does his best work right after a crucifixion.

Good Lord.

Classics from the Republican Reading Room

1945 *by Newt Gingrich*

"I don't think there is going to be a war either, but you seem so sure. What is your big secret? You were so excited about it when you came in here, and now you won't tell me." Suddenly the pouting sex kitten gave way to Diana the Huntress. She rolled onto him and somehow was sitting athwart his chest, her knees pinning his shoulders. "Tell me, or I will make you do terrible things," she hissed.

You know, this nation would be a lot better off if there were more pouty sex kittens and fewer lesbian birth-control-taking working women. There's some debate about whether Newt wrote the dirty bits in this book (which did have a co-author), but we can just see him typing the words "athwart his chest" with his stubby fingers, can't you?

NEWT GINGRICH

Representative from Georgia, 1978–1999; Speaker of the House, 1995–1999

Home wrecker, House wrecker, threat to steal at any time

b. June 17, 1943, Harrisburg, Pennsylvania

CAREER HIGHLIGHT: Forced out Speaker Jim Wright, citing ethics violations, 1989

CAREER LOWLIGHT: Charged with ethics violations, 1995

NICKNAMES: The Speaker; The Pouter; The Cheater; The Conniver

PERSONAL BEST: Brought divorce papers to first wife's hospital bedside

PERSONAL WORST: Cheated on second wife while slamming Clinton's morals

THEME SONG: "Hot for Teacher"

The wandering eye of Newt always wanted more

He's terribly bright, but he's more far right than he is bright. He's become the embodiment of what most Americans hate about right-wingers.

—PAUL BEGALA, 2003

Newt was a young man with a plan—quite simply, to have what he wanted when he wanted it. Oops, make that *who* he wanted when he wanted. Yes, even in high school Newt was too sexy for his Husky Boy pants, vowing as a senior that he'd marry his geometry teacher, Jackie Battley. Sure enough, a year after he graduated, they got married. Years later, after reportedly declaring she wasn't "young enough or pretty enough to be the president's wife," he divorced her. And while he was thoughtful enough to bring the divorce papers to the hospital while Jackie was recovering from cancer surgery, he neglected to pay child support or alimony, forcing their church to take up a collection for his ex-wife and their two daughters. Maybe he was saving up for his next victim: Marianne Ginther. They were happily married in 1981, or at least Marianne thought they were happy. In fact, when Newt announced he'd be leaving the speaker's office in 1998, he proclaimed, "Marianne and I have lots of things to do." But item one on his to-do list was Dump Marianne.

Turned out that unbeknownst to Marianne, but commonly known to much of Washington, Newt had been having an affair since 1995 or so with a young congressional aide named Callista Bistek. You'll be relieved to know that as part of his "defense of marriage" campaign, Newt has made Callista his (third) bride.

You can't have a corrupt lobbyist unless you have a corrupt member of Congress.

—NEWT to Rotary Club, January 4, 2006

And don't think Newt doesn't know what he's talking about. In a staggering display of hypocrisy, Gingrich reacted to the Jack Abramoff lobbying scandal with deep concern. Does he think we've forgotten that he was the captain of the shakedown cruise called the K Street Project? He was there on the maiden voyage, telling every lobbyist in Washington to get on board or be left high and dry when the ship sailed without them. In fact, Newt paired up with Tom DeLay to try to punish a company whose lobbying firm was hiring a Democrat (which earned the Natural one of those "admonishments" from the House ethics panel).

Newt's fancy footwork tripped him up in 1995 over a little thing called GOPAC. It was supposed to be a political action committee for Republican candidates. But it led to charges that it was turning into Newt's personal fund. He didn't bother to register it legally in a number of states. The Federal Election Commission filed a complaint, and the House Ethics Committee began a slow investigation. Good thing the year ended with *Time* magazine making him Man of the Year. (Yeah, we know— Stalin was *Time*'s main man once, too, back in the day.) In 1998 he was cleared of the ethics charges, but he was directed to reimburse the Ethics Committee three hundred thousand dollars. He paid it with money borrowed from Bob Dole.

Newtered: After the GOP suffered its debacle in the 1998 elections, Newt announced that he was resigning as speaker and wouldn't serve another term in Congress. Naturally, he did hang around long enough to vote to impeach Bill Clinton.

HENRY HYDE

Representative from Illinois, 1975–2006

Flame-throwing righty

b. April 18, 1924, Chicago, Illinois

CAREER HIGHLIGHT: Grand Inquisitor in Clinton impeachment hearings

CAREER LOWLIGHT: Clinton acquitted in Senate

NICKNAMES: Plushbottom; Hammerin' Hank

PERSONAL BEST: Voted in favor of assault weapons ban

PERSONAL WORST: Affair with married woman

THEME SONG: "Ma Cherie Amour"

He loved fast women and loose banking regulations

You can't have a virtuous democracy without a virtuous people.
—HENRY HYDE

And you would certainly know, sir. A lot of guys who've played the game have been hypocrites, and a lot of them have been shameless, but Hammerin' Hank Hyde is a standout at being a shameless hypocrite when caught dead to rights. For using the phrase "youthful indiscretion" to refer to a home-wrecking affair he carried on when he was in his forties, Henry is a unanimous choice for the Hall of Shame.

We all remember where we were that day in 1998 when we first learned the news: A woman named Cherie Snodgrass had come forward to say that she'd had a long-term affair with Henry (proving there really is no accounting for taste) years earlier. Whether she was coming forward to call him out for his hypocrisy, or had just reached the bottom of a personal shame spiral, we can't say, but we know we had goose bumps when we heard. After all, Henry was at that very moment leading the impeachment vendetta against Bill Clinton, thundering on about morals and honesty and virtue.

Of course, Henry's reputation wasn't exactly pure as the driven snow before that "youthful" indiscretion was revealed. At the time of the impeachment hearings, he'd just gotten off the hook for his part in the failure of the Clyde Federal Savings Bank, which left taxpayers holding the bag for about sixty-eight million dollars. Henry, who was on the bank board, was one of the people accused of gross negligence, but he maintained he was innocent and refused to pay his part of the settlement that got the federal case dismissed. That case has always been kinda murky to us, especially since Ol' Hank won't tell us why, or even whether, he hired a colorful private eye named Rizzo to find out what one of his political enemies knew about his role in the bank failure. But since Henry is Mr. Virtue, we'll take him at his word that he didn't do it.

Henry was a religious fanatic before being a religious fanatic was cool. Way back in the seventies he began his crusade against women's reproductive rights, and to this day, millions of women consider Henry Hyde Public Enemy Number One. He's the guy who took the first big piece out of abortion rights. In 1976 Congress passed the Hyde Amendment, which cut off federal funds to pay for poor women's abortions. It was just the first of many victories for Hammerin' Hank, who was always looking for a way to score another run for the Crusaders. Luckily, Ronald Reagan came along with a worldview straight out of the Middle Ages. Before long, Henry was leading the charge against the bleeding hearts and peaceniks of the nuclear freeze movement, leaving Ronnie clear sailing for his gigantic arms buildup. And he smiled approvingly as Ollie North and the whole Iran-Contra gang lied to Congress about funneling money to the Contras in Nicaragua. Funny, sometimes a lie is okay, when it's not about something sinful like, say, a blow job.

Speaking of blow jobs, not all of Henry's morals crusades were successful. He tried to pass a law against renting out sexually explicit or violent movies or books to teenagers. (We can just see the pimply-faced Blockbuster clerk being led out in handcuffs for renting *Saving Private Ryan* to some high school kids.) Somehow the nation has survived his failure to get that one through Congress.

Henry is now hanging up his Crusader shield; at eighty-one he's done enough damage. Welcome to the Hall, Hank!

Hall of Shame

BOB DORNAN
CONGRESSMEN

BOB DORNAN

Representative from California, 1977–1997

Righty with reputation for wildness

b. April 3, 1933, New York City

CAREER HIGHLIGHT: Called female political opponents "lesbian spearchuckers"

CAREER LOWLIGHT: Inept presidential campaign ended in abject failure

NICKNAME: B-1 Bob

PERSONAL BEST: Bouncing a check in the House banking scandal . . . to pay for a backyard shrine to the Virgin Mary

PERSONAL WORST: Wife files, withdraws, divorce papers four times

THEME SONG: "Fly Me to the Moon"

Some say he was crazy, others that he was just plain mean

B-1 Bob may be the most misunderstood Hall of Shamer of them all. But that's only because people don't take the time to get to know him. Sure, it's easy to leap to snap judgments about a guy who tried to deny funding for AIDS education, twice tried to get HIV-positive soldiers thrown out of the military, and called a Russian journalist a "betraying, disloyal little Jew." But that wouldn't be fair. And by the way, he calls himself a "shit hot" fighter pilot, not a "shitty" fighter pilot. Just because he happened to crash a fighter jet while in combat over the California desert, and had to eject a couple of other times from fighter jets, that doesn't give critics the right . . . oh, never mind. Some people are just mean-spirited, especially to guys who are too modest to stand up for themselves, like Bob.

He got the nickname "B-1" because of his slavish devotion to funding the B-1 bomber, which was widely believed to be unnecessary, except by the military contractors in his home district. Bob never lost the taste for battle—not with his wife, who accused him in numerous divorce filings of physically abusing her, although she later recanted and blamed her lies on booze and drugs—not with fellow members of Congress, who rebuked him after he said that Bill Clinton had given aid and comfort to the enemy during the Vietnam War—and certainly not with any man who supports a woman's right to choose abortion. Here's what he said about them:

> Men in the pro-choice movement are either men trapped in women's bodies . . . or younger guys who are like camp followers looking for easy sex.

Any fan of TV Land cable television has no doubt caught some of Bob's best work, as Captain Fowler on the classic 1960s show *Twelve O'Clock High*. The nephew of Jack Haley, the Tin Man of Oz, he caught the acting bug early, and even after he hung up his acting shoes and went to Congress, he never lost his taste for props—he reportedly carried a plastic fetus in his pocket for years in case he ran into a plastic woman considering an abortion.

It's very possible that the person he hated most in the world, even more than any abortion provider, was Bill Clinton. He called him a "nerdy flower child," suggested he used cocaine, and referred to him as a triple draft dodger, whatever that meant. He was so appalled when Clinton became president that he decided to mount his own campaign to defeat him in 1996. Sadly, he struck out, collecting zero delegates for his trouble. And while he was busy flaming out as a Republican candidate for president, back home his constituents were being courted by Democrat Loretta Sanchez.

So, after giving up on his quest to run against President Clinton, B-1 Bob came home to run against Sanchez, and lost. But like the brave pilot who never says die, he refused to concede defeat, claiming voter fraud by illegal aliens. Bob insisted on a House investigation, which concluded, after fourteen months, that there had been no voter fraud. Just to prove the point, Sanchez beat him again in 1998, this time by a much bigger margin. Bob tried to make a comeback in 2004, running against another rocket scientist, Naked Republican Dana Rohrabacher. Faced with the impossible choice of a goon versus a loon, voters in the OC went for the goon and turned thumbs down on B-1 Bob.

He's in the Hall now, but bear in mind he's always a threat to dust off his spikes and try for just one more comeback. You've been warned.

DICK ARMEY

Representative from Texas, 1985–2003

Fast-talking, slow-thinking righty

b. July 7, 1940, Cando, North Dakota

CAREER HIGHLIGHT: Majority leader, co-author of the Contract with America

CAREER LOWLIGHT: Loser in power struggle to oust Newt Gingrich

NICKNAME: The Mouth

PERSONAL BEST: Bringing "The Rock" as guest to GOP Convention

PERSONAL WORST: "Barney Fag"

THEME SONG: "Kiss the Frog"

He tried to make trash talk an art form

I've been to Europe once. I don't have to go again.

—DICK ARMEY

Congressional leadership like that makes you proud to be an American, doesn't it? If you had to go through life with a name like "Dick Armey," you'd be a crabby loudmouth, too, so maybe you're thinking you could have a little empathy. Well, don't bother. He'd probably have been an obnoxious trash-talker no matter what his mama named him. This Texas Leaguer earned a place in the Hall of Shame the day he called his colleague, Representative Barney Frank, "Barney Fag." The fact that he immediately tried to take it back and blame the media for reporting his "slip of the tongue" just revealed him to be a coward as well as a bigot.

He was an economics professor when he decided to run for Congress in 1984. In 1994, Newt Gingrich asked him to help write the Contract with America. Dick was a big fan of the flat tax, privatizing Social Security, and saying outrageously ignorant things.

He said Hillary Clinton thought like a Marxist and had Marxist friends. He also told her, "Reports of your charm are overstated."

The "Barney fag" comment was followed by another Barney Frank joke at a party. And as for international relations— it's a rare politician who can outrage both Jews and Arabs, and Dick is a rare politician. In 2002, he had a novel approach for a Palestinian homeland: put it in Sweden, or anywhere except the area generally known as Palestine. He told a shocked Chris Matthews on *Hardball:*

> *Most of the people who now populate Israel were trans-*
> *ported from all over the world to that land and they*
> *made it their home. The Palestinians can do the same,*
> *and we're perfectly content to work with the Palestinians*

in doing that. We are not willing to sacrifice Israel for the
notion of a Palestinian homeland. . . . That's right, I
happen to believe that the Palestinians should leave.

Later, probably after someone explained to him that ethnic
cleansing is not the policy of the United States, he issued a clar-
ification in which he said he wasn't for forcibly evicting Palestinians. Perhaps they can be coaxed to leave, en masse, if Dick
asks them nicely.

But it's not like he's exactly a friend to the Jews, either. At
a round table in Sarasota, Florida, in front of an audience of
mostly Jews, he explained what Jews are really like:

I always see two Jewish communities in America. One
of deep intellect and one of shallow, superficial intellect.
The conservative Jews have a deeper intellect, while the
liberals work in occupations of the heart.

As an equal-opportunity offender, Dick was just as likely to
annoy members of his own party as he was to annoy Democrats. He's believed to have been involved in the failed effort to
shove Newt Gingrich out as speaker in 1997, although it was
his fellow Texan, Tom DeLay, who was the brains behind the
operation.

Sadly, Dick can't count Tom as one of his friends anymore.
He probably can't count on Senator Arlen Specter, another fellow Republican, either. When Dick hung up his cleats to become a (wait for it . . .) high-priced lobbyist, he got into a
tussle with Specter about an asbestos trust fund bill. Good to
see Dick cashing in through the K Street revolving door.

But just because he's retired from public office doesn't
mean we're no longer going to have access to the wit and wisdom of Dick Armey. In a *Wall Street Journal* op-ed in Decem-

ber 2005, he shared his thoughts on the privatization of Social Security:

> *Personally, I've never quite understood the bed-wetters' fears when it comes to personal retirement accounts.*

"Fags," "Marxists," "bed-wetters"—we couldn't be prouder of you, Dick.

Hall of Shame

ROBERT TAFT
GOVERNORS

ROBERT TAFT

Governor of Ohio, 1999–2006

Made the Black Sox scandal look like a Little League barbeque

b. January 8, 1942, Boston, Massachusetts

CAREER HIGHLIGHT: Not getting impeached after pleading guilty

CAREER LOWLIGHT: Considered too insignificant to bother impeaching

NICKNAME: Doofus

PERSONAL BEST: Got into Skull and Bones (like all the Tafts)

PERSONAL WORST: Supported new Jim Crow–like laws in Ohio to suppress black vote

THEME SONG: "I'm a Loser"

He sullied a proud family name for chump change

The Taft family has worked hard to earn a reputation for common sense, for getting things done to help others, and for striving to live up to the highest standards of honesty and personal integrity. . . . And that's the kind of administration I'll lead.

—BOB TAFT, 1999, Inaugural Address

Somewhere, President William Howard Taft is rolling over in his humongous grave. In 2005, his great-grandson, Governor Bob Taft, admitted violating state ethics laws by failing to report gifts and golf outings paid for by others. Bob could have been sent up the river, but he was lucky enough to get off with a small fine.

As the crowds howled for his scalp, demanding he resign or be impeached, tenacious Bob hung in and refused to give ground. He wouldn't step down, although he forced staffers to resign after lesser violations. How could he quit when things were going so well?

The real test for me, really, was whether I could continue to make a difference for the people of the state as Governor.

—BOB TAFT, to the Cleveland *Plain Dealer,* December 23, 2005

That's just what many Ohioans were most afraid of. They thought the real crime was the way he ran their state. Under his leadership, the Buckeye State has become an economic basket case. The record:

- One of the worst unemployment rates in the country.

- Among the slowest rates of job growth.

- A leader in home foreclosures and personal bankruptcies.

Taft's fans especially appreciated some of his dazzling decoy plays, like campaigning to ban gay marriage, and coming up with nifty new license plate slogans like "Choose Life."

Speaking of license plates, we know Governor Doofus goes to bed every night thanking his Lord that he isn't making them in a state penitentiary. If only he'd learned to just say "no" to Tommy Noe, a very prominent Republican fundraiser who has pleaded guilty to illegally funneling thousands of dollars to the 2004 Bush campaign. Somehow Tommy and Taft got to talking, and then playing golf, and the next thing you know, the state has invested fifty million dollars from its Bureau of Workers' Compensation in Tommy's crazy rare-coin fund. They were going to plunk down millions more, until the local newspapers revealed that Tommy had lost about twelve million dollars of the money. Tommy's also been charged with embezzlement, but maybe the money is between the cushions of the couch.

In fact, it was when investigators were searching for the money that they noticed the governor had failed to report gifts and golf outings paid for by Tommy Noe. Hey, he's a busy guy. And he said he was sorry, no, even more than sorry:

"I'm very disappointed in myself," Taft told the judge when he admitted to knowingly filing false income tax returns. The judge ordered him to write a formal apology to the people of Ohio. (Why do we picture Bart Simpson at the blackboard writing "I will not be a sleazy governor" one hundred times?)

We know Bob will hang tough until the bitter end, which comes at the end of his 2006 season. As for what he'll do next, we're thinking maybe a beer distributorship bestowed upon him by a lifelong fan. That seems just right for a descendant of one of America's most storied political dynasties.

He's the first in the Taft family to get into the Hall of Shame, and we think we know just how they're feeling.

Hall of Shame

JOHN ROWLAND
GOVERNORS

JOHN ROWLAND

Governor of Connecticut, 1995–2004

Rose fast, played with abandon, abandoned ethics

b. May 24, 1957, Waterbury, Connecticut

CAREER HIGHLIGHT: Three-time governor of Connecticut

CAREER LOWLIGHT: Lost millions of state dollars in bad Enron deal

NICKNAME: Governor Corrupticut

PERSONAL BEST: Youngest man ever elected governor

PERSONAL WORST: Youngest governor ever forced to resign in disgrace

THEME SONG: "There's a Summer Place"

**He had everything going for him,
but thought he had everything coming to him**

I'm not going to sell my integrity or my twenty-five years of public service for a box of cigars. I mean, it's silly to even think that.
— JOHN ROWLAND, Associated Press interview, May 3, 2004

But if you throw in a Mustang convertible and some free work on your weekend place, now you're talking, right, John?

Big John Rowland was a phenom, a kid when he won his first election. At thirty-seven he was the youngest guy ever elected governor, and his fans reelected him twice. Can you blame him for getting a swelled head, or for turning into an arrogant, greedy liar?

He came from a long line of prominent Connecticut Republicans. They had money, they had power, they had influence. And apparently, they all had nice vacation homes, so Governor Corrupticut decided he wanted one, too, and that's where the trouble started.

As with so many Hall of Shamers, temptations in the off-season were his downfall. John and his wife, Patty, bought a little vacation cottage in 1997. It was a fixer-upper, but John wasn't that handy, so he asked for some help. Free help, as it turned out. From state contractors and government workers. Over the years, that house needed a *lot* of work. You couldn't expect Big John to relax without a hot tub, could you? And the kitchen was a mess, and the heating system, and the ceiling, for gosh sakes.

No work was done on the roof, which may be unfortunate, since the roof fell in on Big John's career when the newspapers started poking around. He paid off an ethics fine for not declaring that he'd taken free vacations at the home of a developer who got big state contracts, and he hoped that would settle things. But that was only the beginning.

When the newspapers suggested maybe he didn't pay for the hot tub and other stuff at the cottage, Big John denied it. Then, two weeks later, he admitted he lied about that. Our favorite part of the whole sordid story was when Patty got up at a luncheon and read a snarky version of "The Night Before Christmas" that blamed the Hartford press for all of her husband's problems:

> I'm late, said Santa, my last stop took hours,
> All that coal I delivered down the Courant's tall towers.
> They used to be good girls and boys, Santa said,
> But the poison pen's power has gone to their head.

You know what they say about the cover-up being worse than the crime? In this case, all things considered, it was about even.

During the scandal Big John continued to deny and defy, but in the end, as the Connecticut House was about to force him to testify under oath as a prelude to impeachment, he gave in and resigned.

The thousands of dollars in improvements on the house were only the beginning. There was a Mustang convertible, champagne, Cuban cigars; and, perhaps taking a page from Duke Cunningham's book, he got somebody to buy his condo in Washington at a wildly inflated price.

Big John copped a plea that allowed him to plead guilty to one count of tax evasion and fraud. He got off with a slap on the wrist—a year in federal prison. He did have to take full blame for what he'd done, and apologize for Patty's bad poetry, too.

We're happy to report that he had to serve only ten months at Loretto Federal Correctional Institution in western Pennsylvania—time off for good behavior. He should have plenty of free time now to do those little fix-it chores around the old vacation place.

BOB LIVINGSTON

Representative from Louisiana, 1977–1999

Right fielder better known for off-the-field antics

b. April 30, 1943, Colorado Springs, Colorado

CAREER HIGHLIGHT: Teammates elect him Speaker of the House

CAREER LOWLIGHT: Immediately forced to resign by sex scandal

NICKNAME: Lover Boy

PERSONAL BEST: Opened multi-million-dollar lobbying firm days after leaving Congress in disgrace

PERSONAL WORST: Bill Clinton ignored his example, wouldn't resign

THEME SONG: "Falling in Love Again"

Proof that cheaters do prosper—big-time

Who can forget where they were when they heard "Livvy" utter these immortal words in December 1998:

> *To my colleagues, my friends, and most especially my wife and family, I have hurt you all deeply and I beg your forgiveness. I was prepared to lead our narrow majority as speaker, and I believe I had it in me to do a fine job. But I cannot do that job or be the kind of leader that I would like to be under current circumstances. So I must set the example that I hope President Clinton will follow. . . .*

Can't you just picture him, the House's version of Lou Gehrig, standing at the microphone to say goodbye? Except that Lou Gehrig had Lou Gehrig's disease, and Bob Livingston had Bob Livingston's disease, the main symptom of which was the inability to keep his pecker in his pants.

Still, it was tragic to see him laid low at the very moment that should have been his greatest triumph. Just as he was about to ascend to the post of Speaker of the House, in stepped the Capitol Hill newspaper *Roll Call* to publish a story about Livingston's extramarital affairs. Livvy knew right then he would not be the speaker; he would not even retain his position on the team. Still, he had treated his fans to a dazzling display of hypocrisy as a moralizing, sanctimonious serial philanderer who had the guts to demand that Bill Clinton resign or face impeachment.

Livvy isn't the first in his family to make it to the big leagues, although he is the first in the Hall of Shame. He had an ancestor who was a senator and secretary of state for Andrew Jackson. Bob wore number 63 in the Livingston family, because he was the sixty-third Robert Livingston in a family that came to America in 1686. And the apple didn't fall far from the tree—one of the Livingstons had a fling with a slave, as Bob learned when his black cousin got in touch with him!

Given his blue-blood background, some scouts doubted he had the arm or the heart to make it in the bigs. But he proved them wrong on his very first day as chairman of the House Appropriations Committee, when he reported for duty with a machete, a bowie knife, and an alligator-skinning knife. On defense, he was able to field campaign contributions effortlessly.

And no one in the modern history of the game made a faster pivot from disgraced congressman to rich and powerful lobbyist than old Number 63. Days after he hung up his cleats, he set up shop on K Street, and within a year he had raked in more than a million dollars. By now, he's making far more.

He was voted onto the Hall of Shame All-Star team in 2003, when he got a billion dollars in U.S. aid for his client, Turkey, even after the Turks refused to let U.S. troops use their turf to invade Iraq, according to the scouts from the watchdog group Public Citizen. Welcome to the Hall, Livvy—you definitely know how to cover all the bases.

11

THE BUSH LEAGUE

GEORGE HERBERT WALKER BUSH

President, 1989–1993

Soft hands, hard heart

b. June 12, 1924, Milton, Massachusetts

CAREER HIGHLIGHT: Elected president of the United States in 1988

CAREER LOWLIGHT: Lost to philandering, draft-dodging hillbilly in 1992

NICKNAME: Poppy

PERSONAL BEST: World War II hero

PERSONAL WORST: Mass pardoning of Iran-Contra criminals

THEME SONG: "Rhinestone Cowboy"

Never afraid to play dirty

Meet the team manager, Poppy Bush! He's the proud patriarch of the whole Bush League brood, including Jeb's "little brown ones," as he lovingly called them. Lanky, limber, and spry, Poppy can still throw a high hard one at a liberal's head when he needs to, and he's not afraid to plunk a pinko if the situation calls for it. Just ask Dukakis.

George learned to play ball at the rough-and-tumble Greenwich Country Day School, competing against inbred upper-class boys whose families had been pillaging the East Coast since the *Mayflower* arrived. He went on to demonstrate his leadership at Phillips Academy, played some ball and joined a fraternity called the AUV, for "Auctoritas, Unitas, Veritas," which was Latin for "Lord, where is that colored boy with our G&T's?"

Unfortunately for his budding baseball career, World War II broke out, and Poppy went straight into the Navy upon graduation. While his father and other relatives were raking in big money as war profiteers, Poppy was a fighter pilot and a decorated war hero. As soon as the war ended, he came back home to marry Barbara Pierce and begin in earnest a life of power and privilege. Like George's father before him, and his dim-witted son W. after, Poppy went to Yale, where he joined the Skull and Bones secret society and captained the baseball team.

After college he moved the family to Texas, where Barbara gradually turned into his grandmother right before his eyes. Using family connections, he started a career in the oil bidness, running a company called Zapata Offshore, which was widely rumored to have been some kind of CIA front. Unlike his sons, he was not an abject failure as a businessman. Politics, however, was another matter. In 1964, Bush ran for the Senate, making an issue of his opponent Ralph Yarborough's support for the 1964 Civil Rights Act. It was a preview of the kind of race-baiting he would perfect in 1988 against Dukakis. He lost to Yarborough, but later was elected to the House of Representatives twice before losing another Senate race.

Luckily, Richard Nixon still liked him, and when he asked Poppy to come in and try to cover his Watergate-besmirched ass, George obliged. As chairman of the Republican National Committee, he obfuscated, justified, and defended Nixon doggedly until the bitter end. For his loyalty he was rewarded with ambassadorships and then made head of the CIA.

Poppy couldn't let all that knowledge of where the bodies were buried (literally) go to waste, so in 1980 he ran for president. Unfortunately, so did Ronald Reagan. It would be eight years of waiting, and begging Bar not to make good on her threat to snap that skinny Nancy like a pencil. Poppy finally got his chance to be president, and of course he made the most of it. Highlights:

- Invading Panama on the kind of flimsy pretext that young Georgie would copy just a few years later. (It was so funny that they called the Panama thing "Operation Just Cause," since when Bar asked why he was overthrowing Noriega, he would shrug and say, "Just 'cause.")

- And then, of course, taking on Saddam to make Kuwait safe for America's oil industry.

- Promising not to raise taxes, and then raising taxes.

If only he hadn't said that "read my lips" thing. If only he hadn't ralphed on that little Japanese fellow's lap in Tokyo. And if only he hadn't misunderstood that when Bar said Quayle was "special," she meant the other kind of special. Oh, well, you can't change the past.

It was a low moment when he lost to a smooth-talking Southern smart-ass like Bill Clinton—good thing he got a mulligan, sort of, when Georgie ran. Nasty business, that Florida thing. Jebby really screwed the pooch. Thank goodness ol' reliable Jim Baker was able to clean up after his boys, until the Supreme Court could fix, er, decide things.

Poppy spends his days now rubbing Georgie's ungrateful nose into his new father-son relationship with Bill Clinton, who turned out to be a nice young man. Very respectful of his elders. George won't forgive W. for saying he consulted a "higher father" about the war in Iraq. "Yeah, who's your daddy now, Georgie," Poppy snickers as he heads off to play golf with the Clinton boy.

Don't worry, Poppy, we don't have to consult a "higher father" to know you're in the Hall of Shame.

GEORGE W. BUSH

Unelected president, 2001–present

Errors at every position, and don't ask him to sacrifice

b. July 6, 1946, New Haven, Connecticut

CAREER HIGHLIGHT: Awarded the presidency despite losing the election

CAREER LOWLIGHT: Choked big-time on 9/11

NICKNAMES: Junior; The First Pinhead; The Decider

ADMITS TO: Conquering a wicked drinking problem

DENIES: Every mistake he ever made, no matter how obvious

THEME SONG: "Fortunate Son"

It is better to be lucky than smart

As much as his teammates resent him, Junior is the smiling captain of the Bush League, hand picked by the Highest Power, his mother Barbara. True, Jeb was the more obvious choice to outsiders who took only intellect, competence, and maturity into account, but Bar saw that Junior had something else to bring to the sacred calling of public service. As the eldest son, he had the pure, undiluted mixture of cluelessness and shamelessness found only in the first dip from the gene pool of the rich and entitled.

Although he fancies himself a Texas cowboy, Junior is actually the product of the old-money Eastern establishment, born and educated in New England. He blossomed into manhood at Phillips Academy in Andover, Massachusetts. There he learned to wield a manly bullhorn, a skill still evident when he finally showed up at Ground Zero a few days after the 9/11 attacks to talk to the rescue and recovery workers there. What were those stirring words?

I hear you . . . and soon some people who had absolutely nothing to do with this attack will hear from all of us.

Or something like that.

He'd come so far from his checkered youth, when he sloshed his way through college, and the next twenty years after that, turning one business venture after another into a steaming pile of failure. We know that his lovely wife Laura got tired of his late-night fact-finding missions in some of Houston's finer cocktail lounges and made him choose between Jack Daniel's and her. But did you know that before there was Laura, there was Cathryn?

True Fact: Boy George was once engaged to a young Houston girl named Cathryn Lee Wolfman. If just hearing that name makes your Jewdar twitch, there may be good reason. She was apparently at least part Jewish, although there's just no way of knowing whether Bar objected to the marriage because of the young lady's unseemly Semitic connection, as Kitty Kelley alleges in her book. Other accounts claim Cathryn broke off the engagement, and it's not hard to imagine her suddenly realizing she could do way better than George and that she'd done nothing to deserve having Barbara Bush as her mother-in-law.

If You Love Someone, Set Them Free...

Junior loved baseball deeply, although he wasn't very good at it himself. He traded away Sammy Sosa, after all, a man who hit more homers in the next ten years than anyone except Barry Bonds. Of all the strings Poppy pulled for him (except the one that he allegedly, some say, although not us, really, pulled to get him into the Guard and away from 'Nam), his favorite was probably the one that helped him buy a small piece of the Texas Rangers with borrowed money. Unlike his other business ventures, the Rangers continue to this day, probably because W.'s had nothing to do with them for years. And proving once again that good things happen to bad people far too often, when the Rangers were sold, Junior made about fifteen million dollars on the deal.

The key to his success, other than the pure luck of birth, is his willingness to be coached, like so many players of limited skill. Whether he's told to go out and pimp a Social Security plan that nobody wants, or to announce a mission to Mars, or to try to explain the legal basis for an illegal wiretap program, he's always game to try.

Sometimes, because teammates can play cruel pranks on one another, the coaches send him out by himself to explain a complicated matter, like why it would be just fine to turn port security over to an Arab company, or the policy of extraordinary rendition, or the latest reason for going to war in Iraq.

Watching him blink frantically at the camera and do that nervous *heh heh heh* chuckle while trying to remember what they've told him to say will put the rest of the team in stitches. But it's all in good fun, and all for the good of one-half of one percent of the country.

Sometimes they let Junior go up to the plate and just swing away, without a coach sending signs. You can always tell when he's on his own—that's when he comes up with a Harriet Miers nomination, or tells a Michael Brown he's doing a heckuva job in New Orleans.

Or when he says he's determined to find out who leaked secret information from the White House to the press:

> *There's just too many leaks. And if there is a leak out of my administration, I want to know who it is. And if the person has violated the law, the person will be taken care of.*
>
> —George W. Bush, September 30, 2003

Oops! He forgot—he was the guy leaking. Scooter Libby says Cheney told him the president wanted him to leak intelligence about Iraq's weapons program to reporters. See? It's like he always says, being president is hard work. There's just too much to remember.

It's highly unlikely that Jeb will ever be able to scrub the stain of incompetence smeared on the family name by his brother's presidency, so we predict Junior will be the last Bush president in our lifetime. He's an odds-on favorite to make the Worst Presidents Ever list. His lasting gift to America may be that he taught us how to laugh through our international shame.

NEIL BUSH

"Businessman"

It's good to be king, but being the Little Prince ain't bad either

b. January 22, 1955, Midland, Texas

CAREER HIGHLIGHT: Mom wrote a Katrina relief check, stipulating that the money has to go to Neil's education software business

CAREER LOWLIGHT: Banned by feds from ever running another bank

NICKNAME: Dry Hole

PERSONAL BEST: Makes honest woman of mistress after messy divorce

PERSONAL WORST: Sex with Asian prostitutes who "just appeared" at his hotel door on multiple occasions

THEME SONG: "Money for Nothing" (tie) "Baby, You're a Rich Man"

Sometimes nice guys do finish first

- If you can fail at an oil company, a gas company, and a savings & loan and still walk away a rich man, *you might be a Bush.*

- If you can earn two million dollars by "working" for a Chinese semiconductor company even though you don't know anything about semiconductors, *you might be a Bush.*

- If you look up "pampered asswipe" in the dictionary and there's a picture of you or a member of your immediate family, *you might be a Bush.*

- And if hookers happen to show up and have free sex with you when you're staying in hotel rooms around Asia, *you just might be Neil Bush.*

(With apologies to our inspiration, Jeff Foxworthy.)

Neil Bush, or "Neilsie" as his mother reportedly calls him, is described by family friends as the one who can complete a sentence. Okay, actually they say he's the most articulate brother, and given how low the verbal bar was set, first by Poppy and then by Neil's brothers, we have no reason to challenge that. Besides, considering how many times Neil has managed to talk rich people out of their money, he probably *is* the articulate one.

Most Americans got acquainted with Neil when the Silverado Savings and Loan went under in 1988. He was one of the directors, and while it is true he certainly wasn't one of the prime decision makers, he did take advantage of his position to send some unsecured loans to some of his business partners. It wasn't just a nice gesture—they were propping up his failing oil company. The government concluded that Neil had numerous conflicts of interest. Ultimately he had to kick in fifty thousand dollars to settle his share of a massive lawsuit.

Usually things work out better for Neil. The old-timers on

Poppy's team have a way of rescuing him when his businesses fail (his oil business, his methane gas business, his S&L), and the family name opens doors, of course. Late in 2005 Neil was seen with an old family friend, the Reverend Sun Myung Moon, traveling around Asia. Rev. Moon, who told U.S. congressmen at an actual Capitol Hill coronation that he is the True Messiah, and also that he had reformed both Hitler and Stalin (he says they're sorry about that whole trying-to-take-over-the-world-and-kill-all-those-people thing). Rev. True Messiah Moon is reported to have given the Bushes lavish lecture fees and campaign contributions over the years. Neil sure keeps wacky company sometimes!

Did we say *wacky*? We meant *tacky*! No offense to the lovely working girls of the Pacific Rim, but what were you thinking? During his divorce proceedings, Neil let fly with a whopper about Asian prostitutes. It seems that on his travels through Hong Kong and other Asian cities, hookers had a way of just showing up at his hotel room, so, naturally, he'd have sex with them. He says he never paid any of them. He was married at the time—maybe that's why. Or maybe it was because Jim Baker wasn't there to reach into his pocket and settle the tab.

Neil is now trying to edumicate America's students, so kids, watch out. He's got a program called Ignite! which he says is a big motivational tool that uses music and cartoons to teach high-schoolers about math and history and the like. Katrina victims now living in Texas will get a chance to try out the program, since Bar just wrote a check to help with their schooling *if* most of the money went to buy Neilsie's software. Here at the Hall, we think the kids don't need to bother studying—just move to Texas and change their names to "Bush."

Welcome to the Hall, Neil. You didn't earn your spot, but hey, what else is new?

JEB BUSH

Governor of Florida, 1999–2006

Played right field and wished there could be a righter field

b. February 11, 1953, Midland, Texas

CAREER HIGHLIGHT: Using mentally retarded rape victim as pawn in anti-abortion battle

CAREER LOWLIGHT: Massive voter suppression still couldn't deliver Florida to his big brother in 2000 without a giant assist from the Supreme Court

NICKNAMES: Mr. November; Governor Purge

PERSONAL BEST: Kept straight face at George's first inauguration

PERSONAL WORST: Tried to send state troopers to "rescue" Terri Schiavo

THEME SONG: "What Is Life"

From the "Sunshine State" to the "Persistent Vegetative State"

When he was growing up, the family always thought Jebby would be president. George was a party boy, Neil was a screwup, and Marvin—hell, which one *was* he, anyway? The boys had a sister, Doro, but girls were expected to be the steely brains behind presidents, not presidents themselves. And Jeb made all the right moves, in the beginning. He was smart enough to get good grades, graduated from the University of Texas Phi Beta Kappa, and get this: *He registered for the draft.* Luckily, his number didn't come up before the war ended. So could this governor be president? We think not.

The fact is he's been mired in so much muck in Florida that even without having to step around the steaming piles of politi-poo left on the trail by his brother, his path to the White House would not be smooth. Among other things, there's the matter of a brain-dead woman. No, not Katherine Harris—this time we're talking about Terri Schiavo, in whose case:

- In the fall of 2003, Jeb ordered doctors who had removed her feeding tube to put it back in.

- Jeb supported state legislation to require the feeding tube to be left in place.

- He sent in state troopers to take her into protective custody, but they were turned away by local police. Jeb was called a traitor by some of the sacred-life mob on the sidewalks.

- But in the whole appalling display, the worst moment came long after Terri was dead and buried. Months later, Jeb ordered prosecutors to investigate Michael Schiavo's actions on the day she collapsed. Jebby found some of the details "troubling." The prosecutors promptly cleared Michael Schiavo.

When the final medical report came in, we weren't sure who the doctors were talking about when they described a brain shrunk to half its normal size—Terri, or Jeb.

Jeb must wonder sometimes if he would have been better off staying in real estate and making a fortune as a private citizen instead of going into politics. He helped his dad lose the Republican presidential nomination to Ronald Reagan in 1980, and after tasting the bitterness of defeat, experienced the sweet taste of setting up business as a Bush. He and his wife, Columba, moved to Florida and he went into real estate while working his way into the state party machine.

Showing the streak of self-entitlement bred into the family for generations, he decided to go for the Big Enchilada and ran for governor in 1994. He lost that race, but now he had the bug. In 1998 he was elected governor of Florida, and that's when the trouble for the rest of us began.

His work in 2000 to help deliver Florida to his brother earned him the nickname Mr. November. You watched Jeb shine (or was it the sweaty face of a cheater who's afraid he's going to be caught?) as he broke new ground in voter suppression, instructing Katherine Harris to disqualify thousands of voters for being black and/or Democrats.

Jeb shares his brother's thirst for religious fascism, but he kicks it old-school Catholic style. He's the family MVP at hardball abortion politics, twice supporting attempts to force mentally retarded rape victims to carry their fetuses to term. One of the women did have an abortion, but the second woman had to continue her pregnancy to term while judges were throwing out Jeb's argument that a fetus is entitled to a court-appointed guardian.

It's a good thing Jebby never said "Read my lips, no offshore drilling." First of all, none of the Bush men actually *have* lips, and secondly, we all know how that phrase worked for

Poppy. But Jeb did fancy himself something of an environmentalist, until he woke up and remembered that Team Bush preserves *profits*, not natural resources. He's been trying to weasel out of a promise to ban offshore oil drilling in the Gulf of Mexico off the Florida coast.

Jeb will retire in 2007 as governor, and he's still thinking about running for president. While it would give Neil a chance to embarrass yet another president, the rest of us are hoping Jeb will just rest on his laurels.

BARBARA BUSH

Manager

She puts the "man" in manager

b. Before they invented dirt

CAREER HIGHLIGHT: First Lady, First Mother, First Enabler

CAREER LOWLIGHT: Mistaken for ghost of George Washington

NICKNAME: Sir

PERSONAL BEST: Developed mothering technique known as "soul deadening," based on scorn and sarcasm

PERSONAL WORST: Expressed fear that Katrina victims would stay in Texas

THEME SONG: "Planet of the Baritone Women"

She'll give you something to cry about

When the League needed a manager, they knew just where to go—up to Kennebunkport, Maine, where the cigar-chomping original Bushwoman, Barbara, was in semiretirement, itching to get back into action. She'd already managed her brood of self-entitled, arrogant whelps into their own big-league careers and she didn't have much to do. Mostly, she'd pick up the phone to ream out the grandkids for following their fathers' paths to DUI citations and recreational drug use. It just wasn't enough. She hungered for the thrill of competition, a chance to make the little people feel even smaller.

Bar was born into a blue-blooded family that dates back to Franklin Pierce, one of America's most forgettable presidents. While still a child of sixteen, she clapped eyes on young George Herbert Walker Bush and fell in love. A year and a half later, they were engaged, he went off to war, and she went to Smith. Bar realized that once she married George, the less she knew, the happier she'd be, so she dropped out of college and dropped into the faded-chintz-lined bubble of upper-class Eastern Republicanism. In no time she was spawning a series of barely literate offspring who, tragically, would become leaders with actual responsibilities. With nothing left to do besides ghost-write books for her dog, Bar pestered Georgie to pull a few strings with the ladies' baseball league. She's been inspiring the girls ever since with her special brand of emotional bulimia.

Bar looks like everybody's grandma (if your grandma wears tungsten Depends), but she's no softie. As manager of a team of frisky females, she's always lecturing the girls about the evils of bikini waxes and dyeing their hair. And any girl who doesn't wear Bar's triple strand of fake pearls with her uniform is automatically sent to Florida and forced to distribute incorrect polling information to voters in "colored" neighborhoods.

"Sir," as her kids affectionately call her, sometimes worries that America will forget her charm, so during the off-season she likes to make personal appearances. After Hurricane Katrina (which Georgie's little librarian wife kept calling "Corinna"), the Manager dropped by the Astrodome to allow the poor unfortunates to bask in her warmth. And yes, she said it was all working out very well for them in Houston. But it wasn't like she burst into singing "Movin' On Up" from *The Jeffersons*, for heaven's sake, even though their situation *was* exactly like that. And the business about saying it was scary that so many of the hurricane "refugees" wanted to stay in Texas . . . well, it *was* scary. She was just saying what all the rich white people were thinking, after all.

Bar, you're first in war, first in peace, and first in the hearts of the League of Their Own. Next up: surpassing your childhood friend Abigail Adams by becoming the mother of *two* presidents. (No, not you, Marvin, for God's sake.) Jeb, she's lookin' at *you*!

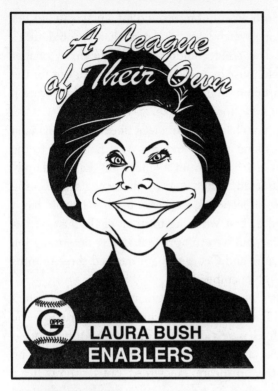

LAURA BUSH

First Lady, 2001–present

Sneaky center fielder forced to play in right

b. November 4, 1946, Midland, Texas

CAREER HIGHLIGHT: Married George W. Bush, quit teaching job

CAREER LOWLIGHT: Heckled by both Muslims and Jews in Mideast

NICKNAME: Buzz Kill

PERSONAL BEST: Convinced voters she liked her mother-in-law

PERSONAL WORST: Fatal car accident as teen kills former boyfriend

THEME SONG: "I'm Trapped"

Incredibly high tolerance for pain

When Bar Bush was hunting around for a playmate for her son W., Laura Lane Welch wasn't what she had in mind, that's for *damn* sure. The child couldn't have come from plainer stock—the Welch house in dusty old Midland wasn't fit for the Bush family's gardening staff. She didn't want her firstborn son to feel he had to *settle*, for pity's sake.

But plucky Laura had her own ideas. She'd been playing in the Texas leagues long enough and saw W. as her ticket to the Show. Here was a rich guy from a fancypants Eastern family who seemed attracted to her. And by the way, *tick tock*—she was on the verge of becoming a spinster teacher. Legend has it he was intrigued at first when he mistook chalk dust on her clothes for cocaine, but we can't prove that. Her determination won Bar over. Laura and George W. got married three months after they met, in November 1977.

It seems every woman wants to change her man once she's snared him, and Laura was no different. You've heard how she got fed up with George's drinking, his alleged use of other recreational drugs, and the occasional DUI, and told him he had to give up the Jim Beam. He agreed, but he threw her a wicked curveball when he became a dry drunk and retained Jesus as his spiritual bartender.

Laura was Mrs. Buzz Kill to him after that, but even George agreed she was right about the booze when he made it to the statehouse as governor of Texas. Laura was always the utility infielder for the Bushes, playing wherever they needed her. One minute she was blathering on about being a teacher/librarian, the next minute she was helping George finish sentences. Before long, Poppy's friends came in and installed some wiring in George's head, and the next thing Laura knew, bingo, he was running for president.

Without Laura, W. never would have made it. She was the defensive star, always pulling off game-saving plays. You'd see her lunging for the twins when they were about to have their pictures taken slurping Crantinis at a T.G.I. Friday's, and then on the next play she was ranging far to her right to convince the freaky fundamentalists that she was a submissive wife who would be second only to Mary as the ideal First Lady. And all the while she kept a sharp eye on George to make sure there were no sips of the Jesus juice.

Winning in 2000 was a team effort, of course, and even then Poppy's friends had to come in and clean up the mess. But it all worked out, and although she's had some awful days in the White House—like when that nasty Cindy Sheehan tries to make her feel guilty about George's war—it's been a lot of fun. And now that the twins are old enough to drink legally, she can relax about opening up a tabloid at the Shop 'n' Save and finding a picture of some dirty hobo holding Jenna's hair while she barfs in the gutter.

Laura, we know you dread retirement, what with having to spend more time with the Bush family and all. But there's a place you're always welcome—where nobody cares whether you enjoy a cocktail or smoke a pack of Winstons. Come 2009, you've got a spot in the Hall of Shame.

KAREN HUGHES

First Nanny

Plays hard, but out of her league in international games

b. December 27, 1956, Paris, France (yes, she is technically a cheese-eating surrender monkey)

CAREER HIGHLIGHT: Creating sales campaign for Iraq war

CAREER LOWLIGHT: Comparing pro-choice advocates to terrorists

NICKNAME: Mom

PERSONAL BEST: Getting reporters off the Bush AWOL and DUI stories during 2000 campaign

PERSONAL WORST: Embarrasses self and country as Ambassador of Making Nice to the Arab World

THEME SONG: "You Spin Me Right 'Round"

Biggest set of balls this side of Barbara Bush

Ambassador Karen Hughes, the Polyester Fog, got her start in the Texas League, where she was a "reporter" for a local television station. There she met the recently dried out George Bush and eventually became his press secretary. Her ability to decoy reporters with trick plays, also called lies, or "spinning," proved to be invaluable to her boss during his first presidential campaign. Karen was a standout in defense when reporters raised questions about the candidate's Lost Year in the Alabama National Guard, and his DUI arrest. Naturally, the Bush team recognized raw talent, and after she skillfully provided cover while the Florida recount was being fixed, she was brought up to the big leagues to play at the White House.

Although she was ready for the Show, the president clearly was not, and it was soon decided that he wouldn't make any decisions beyond which bicycle pants to wear without Karen in the room. (Unfortunately, she didn't travel with him on every PR junket he took in his first year, so she wasn't there to tell him what to do on 9/11 when he learned of the attacks. She would have hustled him out of the classroom, allowing him to take "The Pet Goat" with him so he could learn how it came out.) When he finally did speak to Karen, she told him to be brave and come home, because she thought the American people should hear from their "leader" on 9/11, not realizing how much scarier that would make it for people who had suffered such a shock already. She was always at his side as his number one bench jockey—until July 2002, when her fans and her president listened in disbelief as "Mom" announced she had to go back home to Texas and be a mom, of all things. The Bush team reeled at the loss of their MVP, and the president persuaded her to come back to D.C. regularly to help the Decider make decisions.

Just months later, her old team called her back for the World Series of obfuscation: selling the American people and the world on the war in Iraq. As part of the White House Iraq

Group, she helped develop a marketing plan to sell America on the idea that killing thousands of civilians in Iraq would make us safer at home. Some of their finest work involved getting the whole administration to use the phrase "the smoking gun could turn out to be a mushroom cloud" when they talked about Saddam trying to nuke the bejeezus out of us. And Americans bought the war like a new brand of detergent. Hey, don't blame Karen for the thing getting all screwed up; her job was to create a market for the war, not to fight it.

"Mom" went back to being a mom, and even had time to write her "memoirs" (and we use that term in the post–James Frey sense). *Ten Minutes from Normal* was what she called them, although *Ten Miles from Truth* might have been more accurate. In fact, it was on a book-tour interview on CNN that she made a connection between pro-choice activists and terrorists:

> *The fundamental difference between us and the terror network we fight is that we value every life. It's the founding conviction of our country, that we're endowed by our creator with certain unalienable rights, the right to life and liberty and the pursuit of happiness.*

After removing her Size 10 Easy Spirit from her mouth to say she didn't mean what she obviously meant, Karen was called back up to the bigs one more time, to help her president get reelected. With her usual bag of tricks, including questioning the military service of John Kerry, she helped persuade a reluctant nation to vote for Bush.

Now she's working her magic on the Arab world, as Ambassador of Why They Hate Us. Her first "listening tour" was roundly denounced as an appalling failure, perhaps even doing more harm than good. She seemed to actively alienate the

Muslim women she was trying to win over, and managed to be caught in several whoppers by the American press traveling with her. For the record, Mom, the phrase "under God" does not appear anywhere in the U.S. Constitution, and telling the Muslim world it does only makes them more suspicious that your beloved president is on a crusade for Jesus. But don't feel bad—everybody strikes out sometimes. You'll always be the Bush League's designated hitter.

Classics from the Republican Reading Room

SISTERS *by Lynne Cheney*

We would love to know what Lynne Cheney was thinking when she wrote her prairie lesbian novel, *Sisters*. Suffice it to say that in this hot, steamy 1981 novel of the love that (in the Cheney house) still dares not speak its name very much, sisters were doing it for themselves, to quote Annie Lennox.

The women who embraced in the wagon were Adam and Eve crossing a dark cathedral stage—no, Eve and Eve, loving one another as they would not be able to once they ate of the fruit and knew themselves as they truly were. She felt curiously moved, curiously envious of them. She had never to this moment thought Eden was a particularly attractive paradise, based as it was on naïveté, but she saw that the women in the cart had a passionate, loving intimacy forever closed to her. How strong it made them. What comfort it gave.

LYNNE CHENEY

Righty who wanted to rewrite history . . . literally

b. August 14, 1941, Casper, Wyoming

CAREER HIGHLIGHT: Head of National Endowment for the Humanities

CAREER LOWLIGHT: Unable to burn all objectionable books

NICKNAME: Big Sister

PERSONAL BEST: Conceived in time to get Dick a draft deferment

PERSONAL WORST: Faked outrage at discussion of gay daughter

THEME SONG: "Don't Know Much About History"

Second Lady, First Nag: Big Sister is watching you

Lynne Ann Vincent always knew she was destined for big things. Of course, growing up in Casper, that could mean having your own Mary Kay cosmetics franchise, but Lynne's eyes were on an even bigger prize. She wanted to be powerful. There was only one boy in high school who shared her vision, and that was young Dick Cheney, who tried to curl his lip like Elvis but ended up just looking like a snarly bastard.

He wasn't exactly ideal—he was "asked to leave" Yale, came home and got into trouble with the law (two DUIs,) but she saw in young Dick a guy who was really going places. (Except Vietnam, of course.) They married in 1964, and she got pregnant just in time to help Dick qualify for deferment number five. They settled into a married life marked by huge quantities of Lynne's artery-clogging meals, with their two lovely daughters, Elizabeth and Mary. (Mary is a lesbian and they're very proud of her but for God's sake never speak of it in public or Lynne will have you arrested. You got that, bee-yotch?)

In between driving Dick home from various cardiac emergencies and spending quality minutes with the girls, Lynne led a busy life, but it wasn't quite fulfilling enough. She was looking for a new challenge, so when the League came calling, she couldn't resist.

We can just imagine how a teammate might have remembered her: "Sometimes it was hard to tell which team Lynne was playing for. She'd come off like the Church Lady, you know, lecturing us about keeping our knees locked together when we sat on the bench. But then on long bus rides she'd read out loud to everybody from one of her dirty novels. I guess our favorite was *Sisters*, what with its hot girl-on-girl love scenes. Lynne could be real mean and acted like she was smarter than everybody else, but that girl could write about love." (Note: You people do realize we made this quote up, right?)

Lynne's playing career was cut short when Dick was

elected to Congress. While he was learning integrity from a series of Republicans beginning with President Nixon and Donnie Rumsfeld, Lynne was planting her success tree. Finally, dear old Ronald Reagan appointed her to her dream job, as head of the National Endowment for the Humanities. It was there that she was able to expose the whole Hate America First version of history that was polluting our children's minds with all those unnecessary facts about Native Americans and slavery and the like.

Ultimately, Lynne felt compelled to write her own version of American history—over and over again. She has churned out children's books in a prose style often described as punitive, and her books are a special favorite among the home-schooling movement.

These days she's busy correcting more recent American history. Lynne spends lots of time telling increasingly skeptical audiences that her husband did *not* link Saddam Hussein to 9/11, no matter what they saw and heard him say on *Meet the Press*. It did not happen. It's just like all that nonsense about rounding up the Japanese during World War II, or taking land away from the Indians.

With so many textbooks to change, Lynne can't imagine a day when she'll retire. But the girls have gotten together and voted her into the Hall of Shame anyway. The League of Their Own says howdy, Sister!

A League of Their Own

HELEN CHENOWETH

CONGRESSWOMEN

HELEN CHENOWETH

Representative from Idaho, 1995–2001

She never met an endangered species she didn't want to eat

b. January 27, 1938, Topeka, Kansas

CAREER HIGHLIGHT: Described nonwhites as the "warm-climate community" who don't like the weather in Idaho

CAREER LOWLIGHT: Hit with dead salmon by environmentalist

NICKNAME: Salmon Patty

PERSONAL BEST: Campaigned as moral values candidate

PERSONAL WORST: Forced to admit to affair with married man

THEME SONG: "I'm Easy (Like Sunday Morning)"

> **Keeping date-rape drugs safe from government intrusion**

She was Idaho's sweetheart from January 1995 to 2001. Unfortunately, for six years she was also Vern Ravenscroft's sweetheart, while he was married to someone else. The affair was revealed in the middle of the battle over the impeachment of Bill Clinton, while Helen was running an ad that said:

> *Bill Clinton's behavior has severely rocked this nation and damaged the office of the president. I believe that personal conduct and integrity does matter.*

Although apparently grammar don't.

Timing is everything in baseball and in the politics of personal destruction. It's true the revelation was a high hard one that sent her briefly to the deck. But she dusted herself off and came up with the perfect response:

"I've asked for God's forgiveness, and I've received it," she reported. Mrs. Ravenscroft was another matter. "I don't see how Helen can live with herself and do this," she told the local newspaper.

Helen had balls, for sure. In the space of a few weeks, she racked up votes against funding for child-abuse prevention, against funding for poison-control centers, and against a ban on a date-rape drug. She was adamantly opposed to government intruding on people's lives, apparently even when they're unconscious and being gang-raped in a Boise bar.

When she wasn't busy shutting down poison-control centers, Helen was on the lookout for Communists getting to our borders through the Panama Canal. Even though the crowds laughed at her, she doggedly spoke out against the handover of the canal to Panama's control. Who but Helen would maintain that if the United States turned over control of the canal, it would become a staging area for Red China, right under our noses?

Helen didn't have a lot of experience with Panamanians, or

with anybody from Central or South America, for that matter. Her home team, the Idaho Aryans, were all white, and she said that was because of nature. Blacks and Hispanics are "warm-climate people," she explained, and besides, Idaho doesn't grow the kinds of crops Hispanics like to pick.

When it came to bizarre statements, Congressman Helen (she wanted to be called "congressman") had a million of them. Like how the only endangered species is the white Anglo-Saxon male. And right after the Oklahoma City bombing, she was quoted as saying, "While we can never condone this, we must look at the public policies that may be pushing people too far."

Huh? Well, she may not be smart, but she is a tough cookie. Helen was famous for saying that she couldn't understand how salmon could be endangered when you could buy canned salmon in the grocery store. An environmentalist responded by throwing a big dead salmon at her at a congressional hearing in Montana. Time was called so she could pick the dead fish out of her hair, but she stayed gamely (pun intended!) through the hearing. That's our girl.

Helen found out just how popular she was in 1996, when she faced a last-minute challenge from a Republican newcomer, a doctor named William Levinger. During the taping of an interview at a Boise television station, Levinger announced that he was running for Congress because he couldn't swim to Hawaii. He further offered the reporter five thousand dollars in cash to kiss him, and then stripped off most of his clothes. Police led him away in handcuffs when he refused to leave.

Levinger spent several weeks in a mental institution, returning to the campaign just in time for the election. He still managed to get 32 percent of the vote against Helen. (She went on to defeat her Democratic opponent by a narrow margin after outspending him two to one.)

Helen hung up her cleats in 2001, keeping her promise to term-limit herself. For her work as a moralistic, sanctimonious hypocrite, she was a unanimous first-round choice for the Hall of Shame. The League of Their Own is proud of you, Helen!

CHRISTIE TODD WHITMAN

Governor of New Jersey, 1993–2001; EPA chief, 2001–2003

Star center fielder, goat in right field

b. September 26, 1946, New York City

CAREER HIGHLIGHT: First woman governor of New Jersey

CAREER LOWLIGHT: Dressed in undercover-cop drag, frisked a teenager accused of Driving While Black for cheesy photo op

NICKNAME: The Spine

PERSONAL BEST: Dedicated Howard Stern rest stop on New Jersey highway

PERSONAL WORST: Told people near Ground Zero that toxic air was safe

THEME SONG: "I Can't Make You Love Me"

> **Ultimate team player for a team that didn't want her**

No EPA administrator has ever been so consistently and publicly humiliated by the White House.

—PHIL CLAPP, President, National Environmental Trust,
to *Salon*, May 22, 2003

Christie learned to play ball on the Todd family's estate "Pontefract" (a Latin word meaning "smell that old money") in the rolling hills of New Jersey. As a little girl she spent hours shagging fungoes hit to her by the family's butler and groundskeepers. Noting her talent, her father, a multimillionaire builder with ties to the Rockefeller family, sent her to hone her skills at private schools in Paris and Switzerland. Like so many athletes, she continued to be influenced by her father, who became New Jersey GOP chairman during her formative years.

Playing triple-A ball as governor of New Jersey from 1994 to 2001, Christie played center field, able to cover left and right field when necessary. As the star of the Rockefeller Republicans, she played by old-school rules which stipulated players would be social moderates and fiscal conservatives. Attempting to show real range to her right, she famously rode with police in Camden, New Jersey, and had her picture taken frisking a drug suspect. Even she admitted it was a bonehead play.

In 1994 she was scouted by Newt Gingrich and brought up to the Show to deliver the response to Bill Clinton's State of the Union address. In 1996, she co-chaired the Republican convention with George W. Bush, and in 2001, he picked her to head the Environmental Protection Agency.

Trouble was, Bush's team didn't trust her. She was all tweedy and rich, for one thing, and they thought she was stuck-up. Plus she was practically a Communist.

Her new team stranded her in center, pretending she wasn't even there. They trash-talked her in the locker room, and there were ugly incidents involving Ben-Gay in her athletic gear, but most League observers think she never recovered from the political beaning she suffered, a high hard one right in the melon that sent her reeling. The fact that it came from her own pitcher made it even worse.

Christie was at bat, with the real Washington Senators hanging on her every word, talking about how global warming was a fact and how she had a game plan for playing by the Kyoto rules. All of a sudden, *pow!* The president says screw Kyoto, I'm not convinced global warming exists. And down she went. She never quite recovered from the embarrassment.

There were plenty of stories about her off-the-field battles with management, but on the field she did what she was told. Her teammate Colin Powell told her she was getting blown around so much she reminded him of a wind dummy, one of those effigies the military throw out of a plane to check the wind over a landing zone.

There was the time early on when the administration wanted to relax the standards for arsenic in drinking water and sent Christie out to defend the decision. Then, when the press went crazy, they sent her back out to say they wouldn't change the standards after all. That was awkward.

But Christie's fans will always remember her greatest clutch performance, days after 9/11, when she told residents of the neighborhood around the World Trade Center that the air was just fine to breathe. The fact that nobody knew whether it was or not didn't matter—her team needed her to say it. When it turned out to be untrue, Christie had a novel defensive play—she said if folks had just worn their protective gear, they wouldn't have gotten so sick.

Christie "The Spine" Whitman finally hung up her spikes in June 2003 to write a book about her experiences. For those expecting a *Ball Four*–style tell-all, it was a huge disappointment, more like "tell-nothing." It was called *It's My Party, Too*, and it's obvious that her former teammates are perfectly happy to let her cry if she wants to.

GALE NORTON

Interior Secretary, 2001–2006

When it's time to take the field, she does . . . literally

b. March 11, 1954, Wichita, Kansas

CAREER HIGHLIGHT: First female Secretary of Interior

CAREER LOWLIGHT: Failed effort to personally take over endangered species designations

NICKNAME: Gale Force

PERSONAL BEST: Called "James Watt in a skirt"

PERSONAL WORST: Lobbyist for lead-paint company that was sued numerous times for polluting

THEME SONG: "This Land Is *So* Not Your Land"

The Natural Disaster

Good riddance.

> —RODGER SCHLICKEISEN, president, Defenders of Wildlife

I hate to see her go.

> —KATHY HALL, Colorado Oil and Gas Association

Gosh, it seems Gale Norton's retirement from the League, after five years as secretary of the interior, provoked something of a mixed reaction.

Fans called her Gale Force, because when she was around, nothing in the park was safe. During her five glory years at Interior, coal mining increased 22 percent on public lands, and natural-gas production was up nearly as much. As for cleaning up her own environment, it will be up to prosecutors to determine whether our Gale's department was polluted by Jack Abramoff money.

Gale spent eight years as Colorado attorney general before getting called up to the big leagues. She quickly showed her talent for playing by the rules, as long as they were written by industry. Environmentalists called her the Polluter's Dream, and the polluters called her Gale. Colorado fans remember her best defensive move, which was to sit on her hands as a mining company polluted a river, a power plant fouled the air, and a logging company conducted illegal midnight burns. She learned all her tricks from James Watt, who was the pro-business, anti-environmentalist interior secretary for Ronald Reagan until he had to resign after making a remark that managed to offend almost everybody. Some people called her "James Watt in a skirt," and we're sure she considers it a compliment. He probably does, too.

Gale was a force of nature in her next job as a lobbyist for a company called NL Industries, which used to be called the National Lead Company. (Gee, why didn't they just call it "Poisons 'R' Us"?) As you might expect, they had a lot of lawsuits on their hands from people who accused them of poisoning their kids. The federal government was suing NL, too. The same federal government that was about to employ Gale, come to think of it. That was cozy, wasn't it?

Gale liked to play with all kinds of teammates, so it's no surprise that she and taxophobe Grover Norquist teamed up to form the Council of Republicans for Environmental Advocacy, or CREA. To cynics it seemed like a good place for polluters to send contributions, and CREA did get a lot of their money from the chemical and logging industries. Some environmentalists went so far as to call it a front for polluters. But that's only because they'd never heard of Jack Abramoff.

Kids, you remember Black Jack Abramoff, don't you? Sure you do. So you'll be interested to learn that Mr. Abramoff had his Indian tribe clients send hundreds of thousands of dollars to CREA. Now, why would he do that?

Well, we can't be sure, but we do know that Gale Norton was interior secretary at that time, and she had a lot of power over Indian casinos. Remember all those congressmen and congresswomen who wrote her letters asking her not to approve a casino that would have competed with casinos run by Abramoff's clients? And we also know that the nice lady who took over CREA, a gal named Italia Federici, talked to Gale's assistants in the Interior Department a lot and seemed downright eager to be helpful to Abramoff's clients. It sure feels like there's something fishy going on, but hey, Gale says Abramoff had nothing to do with her decisions. She's not under any kind of investigation.

Gale has put Washington behind her and is enjoying retirement. She has plenty of things to do besides burn copies of photos taken of her with Jack Abramoff.

Gale, we've got your spot in the Hall all picked out. Oh, but don't drink the water from the fountain near your plaque. There was just a little mining spill upriver, and the folks who run the mine haven't had a chance to clean it up yet. We know you wouldn't want to rush them.

THE PARTY'S OVER

The Naked Republicans exposed in these pages certainly didn't invent greed or corruption. Greed is one of the main reasons people join the GOP, after all. Who but a Republican like Tom DeLay would be able to say with a straight face that nothing is more important in the face of a war than cutting taxes? These guys are like the looters at Baghdad's national museum, carrying off their society's treasures while Donald Rumsfeld shrugs and says "Stuff happens." Secret earmarks for their big donors, influence peddling, lavish gifts and trips, and cash, cash, cash. And it turns out our CEO president learned his management skills from Enron.

Kind of ironic, isn't it, that the guy most likely to send a slew of these greedy bastards to jail is one of their own—Black Jack Abramoff, who's pointing fingers and naming names? It's almost as if somebody up there is paying attention.

Hey, maybe there's something to this intelligent design thing, after all. One look at the polls might make a believer out of anybody.

With Republican candidates running away from the president as if he had the bird flu, it's obvious that they can smell the disaster coming. No problem—call FEMA for help. They're good at disasters.

It's going to take a Hazmat team years to clean up the toxic sleaze on Capitol Hill, and the sooner they start, the better off we'll all be. So, ladies and gentlemen of the Greedy Old Party, it's time to put your clothes back on and go home.

ACKNOWLEDGMENTS

A great big thank-you to my great friend and adviser, Laurie Liss; to my wonderful editor, Julia Cheiffetz; to David Bender, who helped shape this idea and make it all work; and to the brilliant Vanessa Silverton Peel, whom I would trust with my life. The caricatures are the work of the incredibly talented Dave Counts, whose toostupidtobepresident.com is a website guaranteed to cheer you up. Thanks also to my husband, Dennis Kardon, who laughs at my jokes if I insist, and sometimes even when I don't, and to my daughter, Julia Kardon, who loves good books but will like this one anyway. Also thanks to my parents, who always encouraged me to write a book, though not necessarily one like this.

ABOUT THE AUTHOR

SHELLEY LEWIS was born and grew up deep in the heart of hostile Red State territory—Omaha, Nebraska. At an early age she was embraced by an elite, super-secretive society known as Liberals. She graduated from New York University's School of the Arts and spent several decades as a writer and executive producer of news programs for Mainstream Media, working at two of the three major networks and a certain Cable News Network, until she'd finally had enough and left the MSM to co-create and launch Air America Radio. Some of her best friends are conservatives. She and her husband, Dennis Kardon, live in New York City.